The 8th Air Force
Victory and Sacrifice

The 8th Air Force Victory and Sacrifice

A World War II Photo History

John W. Lambert

Schiffer Military History
Atglen, PA

Acknowledgments

U.S. Army Air Force personnel took the vast majority of the photos displayed in this volume. Not all official photos taken during the course of the war reached the archives now located at College Park, MD. Of those that can be found in the "USAF Collection," many had cryptic or erroneous data. Extensive research was necessary in order to determine the date, locale, units involved, and fate of men and aircraft. A few scenes taken inside Germany were obtained after the armistice, and are also part of the USAF Collection. All of these pictures are in the public domain.

Some remaining few photos used herein came from the private collections of veterans and history buffs in the U.S. and Europe because of their generosity and desire to share history. For use of those images and research data we are indebted to: Bob Dorr, Robert Elliott, Wally Forman, Robert Foose, Garry Fry, John Gray, Axel Kornführer, Ed Kueppers, Mike O'Brien, Merle Olmsted, Tom Perry, and Sam Sox.

When viewing these scenes, it is important to remember that all were taken some 60 years ago. Many of the action photos are slightly blurred, as they could not be staged.

The Eighth Air Force was composed of bomber and fighter commands, and these were additionally fragmented into subordinate air divisions and combat wings. The senior organizations existed to structure and administer the vast Eighth. The basic combat unit that we use to identify various scenes is of numbered groups and squadrons, each bomb group containing four squadrons, each fighter group three. For more detailed research, look to unit histories, many of which are in print, or on the web.

Dedication

This volume is dedicated to all those who served in the Eighth Air Force in World War II, living and dead. It was assembled for the benefit of their descendents and future generations of Americans so that, in visualizing these scenes and looking on the young faces, they might comprehend the incredible sense of duty of these intrepid men who repeatedly faced death's catalogue of horrors. Bless them all.

And a very personal dedication to my technical advisor, mentor for this work, and long time friend, Capt. Michael A. O'Brien, 489th Bomb Group, Eighth Air Force. As part of that great generation he served 25 missions over the tortured skies of Europe from the left seat of a B-24 Liberator.

They shall not grow old, as we that are left grow old:
Age shall not weary them nor the years condemn.

Lawrence Binion

Book Design by Ian Robertson.

Library of Congress Control Number: 2006927486

Printed in China.
ISBN: 0-7643-2534-5

We are interested in hearing from authors with book ideas on related topics.

Published by Schiffer Publishing Ltd.
4880 Lower Valley Road
Atglen, PA 19310
Phone: (610) 593-1777
FAX: (610) 593-2002
E-mail: Info@schifferbooks.com.
Visit our web site at: www.schifferbooks.com
Please write for a free catalog.
This book may be purchased from the publisher.
Please include $3.95 postage.
Try your bookstore first.

In Europe, Schiffer books are distributed by:
Bushwood Books
6 Marksbury Avenue
Kew Gardens
Surrey TW9 4JF, England
Phone: 44 (0) 20 8392-8585
FAX: 44 (0) 20 8392-9876
E-mail: Info@bushwoodbooks.co.uk.
Visit our website at: www.bushwoodbooks.co.uk
Free postage in the UK. Europe: air mail at cost.
Try your bookstore first.

Contents

Introduction

One of the most bitterly contested battlefields of World War II was the air over Western Europe. From 1942 through 1945 thousands of aircraft engaged in daily combat, weather permitting, as the Allies attempted to destroy Germany's war-making capability, and the Germans sought to defend Occupied Europe and the Fatherland.

Bomber Command of the British Royal Air Force began attacking German targets in 1939. They suffered heavy losses in daylight whenever missions took them beyond the range of escorting fighters, compelling a change to night raids. These night formations were strung out, bombing by radar, or aiming at the fires set by pathfinders. By 1942 RAF night attacks, employing thousand-plane operations and incendiary bombs, were acknowledged as saturation bombing. The strategy was to destroy German industry, along with the urban centers that housed the factories and workers.

When the Americans arrived in England in 1942 to join in the strategic air offensive, they brought with them an untested doctrine of high altitude daylight precision bombing. The prewar U.S. Army Air Forces had been dominated by bomber men, and advancing bomber design convinced them that their tightly packed formations of four-engined heavies could defend themselves beyond the range of escorting fighters, and with the new Norden bombsight, drop on their intended target with a high degree of accuracy. American airmen spoke of hitting a pickle barrel from 25,000 feet. The British scoffed at the daylight concept, but nonetheless lent their support to the establishment of the Eighth Air Force. This strategic air force building in East Anglia, and the smaller Fifteenth Air Force operating from Italy, would swell to 1,000-plane armadas. Combined with the RAF, they ultimately laid waste to Hitler's war machine and many German cities.

British and American bombing tactics remained distinctly different, but military leaders of both nations soon agreed on target priorities for what was called the "combined bomber offensive." The German air force, the Luftwaffe, was at the top of that list. Other major targets were transportation, the power grid, oil refineries, submarine bases and construction yards, and heavy industry.

Still, German resistance was greater than the military planners could have possibly realized, and German ability to repair and adapt their strategic industrial complex was a marvel of ingenuity. Luftwaffe fighters and anti-aircraft batteries proved more effective and more resilient than anticipated. By the fall of 1943 Eighth Air Force bomber losses in deep, unescorted raids were so severe that operations were suspended until long-range fighters could become available.

The air war dragged on for another two years and, although the Allies eventually prevailed, the Eighth Air Force was engaged in a war of attrition that produced staggering losses. When World War II mercifully ended in mid-1945, the Eighth had suffered the loss of over 8,500 aircraft, and more combat casualties than any other numbered U.S. military unit.

Other historical works (see bibliography) have documented the detailed combat operations of the Eighth Air Force. In this volume we seek to provide an historical image of the campaign over Western Europe utilizing a gallery of representative photos to describe the nature of aerial combat some six decades ago.

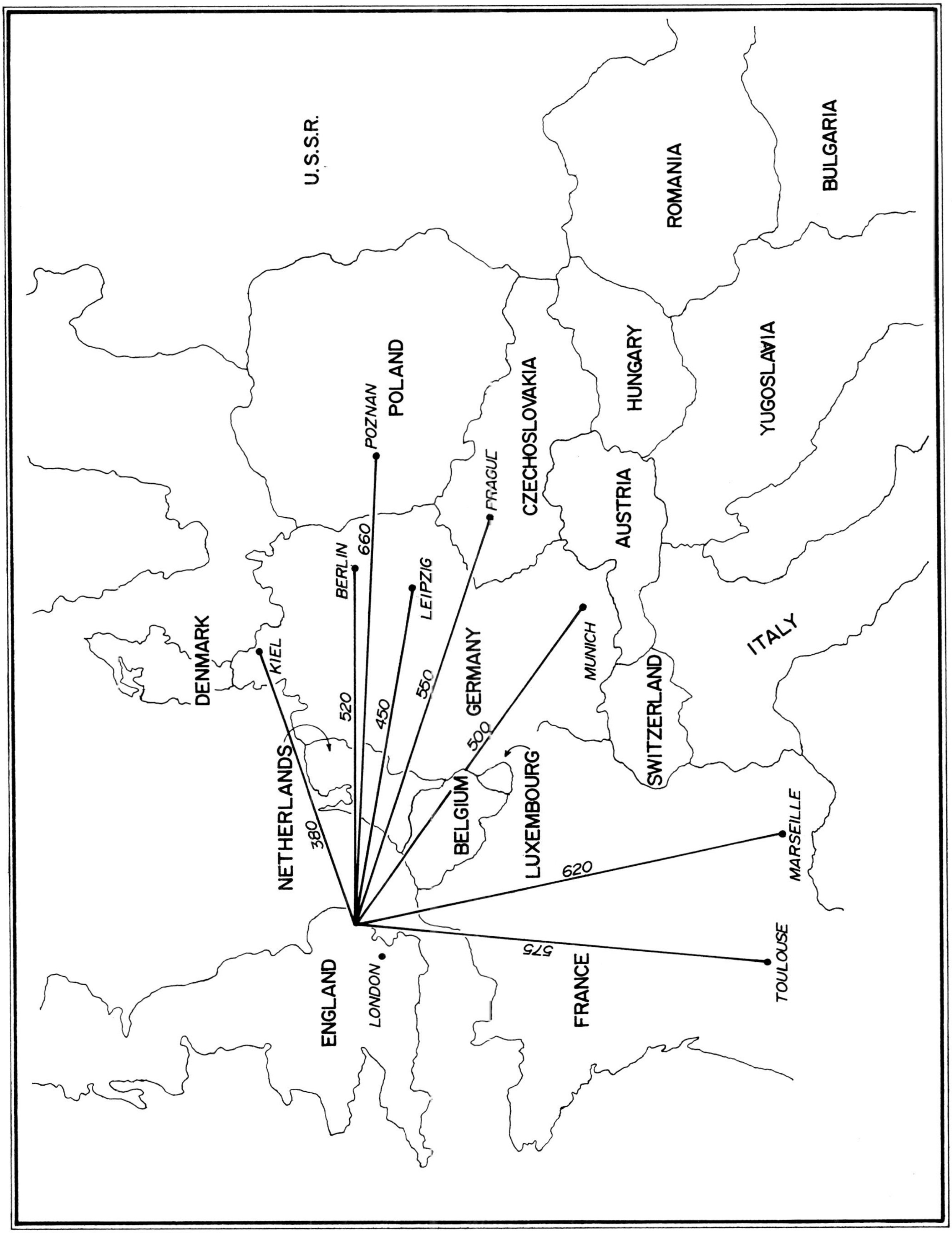
U.S.S.R.
ROMANIA
BULGARIA
POLAND
POZNAN
HUNGARY
YUGOSLAVIA
CZECHOSLOVAKIA
PRAGUE
AUSTRIA
BERLIN
660
LEIPZIG
DENMARK
KIEL
GERMANY
550
520
450
MUNICH
ITALY
SWITZERLAND
500
NETHERLANDS
LUXEMBOURG
BELGIUM
380
620
MARSEILLE
ENGLAND
LONDON
FRANCE
575
TOULOUSE

1

The Strategic Mission

The initial high altitude heavy bombardment missions by the Eighth Air Force were modest probes by handfuls of Boeing B-17 aircraft against military targets in Occupied France. The 97th Bomb Group inaugurated the strategic air campaign against the enemy with a 17 August 1942 attack on Rouen's railway yards, followed by airfield strikes, with the 301st and 92nd Bomb Groups.

RAF Spitfires escorted some of these early shallow probes into France, thus losses were modest. By the start of 1943 five more bomb groups had arrived in England and become operational, and two of the original groups, the 97th and 301st, departed for North Africa to become the nucleus of the Fifteenth Air Force.

The Eighth Air Force received its own fighter unit in October 1942 with acquisition of the American Eagle Squadrons, volunteers to the RAF. Designated the 4th Fighter Group, it continued to operate Spitfires until Republic P-47s arrived in England. The P-47 equipped 56th and 78th Fighter Groups followed in April 1943. But these aircraft also lacked the range for escort deep into Germany.

Early bombing results, coupled with outlandish claims for the destruction of enemy fighters, caused Eighth Air Force commanders to believe that they could achieve their goals with a loss ratio of just four percent of the aircraft dispatched.

However, as the experiment in daylight bombing proceeded into the summer of 1943, and the bombing missions went beyond the range of the P-47s into Germany, reality set in. The loss ratio rose steadily to eight percent, and then ten percent. On 17 August 1943, during a raid on Schweinfurt/Regensburg, German fighter and flak defenses caused the loss of 60 B-17s. The same target was attacked again on 14 October with another 60 B-17s shot down, for a combined loss ratio of 22 percent. Fourteen additional B-17s had been forced down at sea or crash-landed in England. Over 1,300 aircrew members were killed, wounded, or missing in action from the two deep penetrations.

The daylight bombing campaign had, according to the official AAF history, "reached a crisis. The cost had risen alarmingly while bombing success had remained problematical." And despite claims for the destruction of enemy fighters, intelligence showed that the German fighter force had not diminished, and aircraft production had increased.

The critical need was for long-range escorts. Early P-47 fighters had a 300 mile range, augmented to near 400 miles with disposable wing tanks; and the P-38 had a 450 mile range, augmented to 585 with two 108 gallon drop tanks. When the P-51 arrived on the scene late in 1943 it had an escort range of over 600 miles.

There would be another year and a half of bitter aerial warfare over Europe, but with 1944 the loss ratios of the Luftwaffe increased, while bomber losses for the Eighth Air Force peaked, then steadily improved. By 1945 American bomber and fighter production swelled Eighth Air Force strength to 40 bomb groups and 15 fighter groups. The U.S. also had a seemingly endless supply of replacement aircrews, while the Germans suffered the irreplaceable loss of veteran Luftwaffe fliers.

B-17 Flying Fortresses of the pioneer 306th Bomb Group arrive over their target in Occupied Europe. The nearest Fort stays on course to salvo its bomb load even though the #3 engine is smoking from flak damage. (USAF)

A formation of B-17s from the 390th Bomb Group unload their deadly cargo of high explosive bombs. These aircraft are dropping by use of a device called an intervalometer, causing the bombs to release "in train." The setting of the intervalometer is dependent on the ground speed of the aircraft and the desired spacing of the bomb bursts on the target. (USAF)

The bomber crews had a saying that sometimes the flak was, "so thick you could get out and walk on it." This must have been that sort of situation. Intense heavy AA bursts seem to bracket a 452nd Bomb Group B-17 over Ludwigshafen, Germany, in September 1944. (USAF)

A formation of B-17s of the 91st Bomb Group at 24,000 feet over northern Germany. These tight formations allowed the Eighth Air Force heavy bombers to provide mutual support against German fighter attacks. However, the close formations were more vulnerable to the box barrages of German anti-aircraft guns. (USAF)

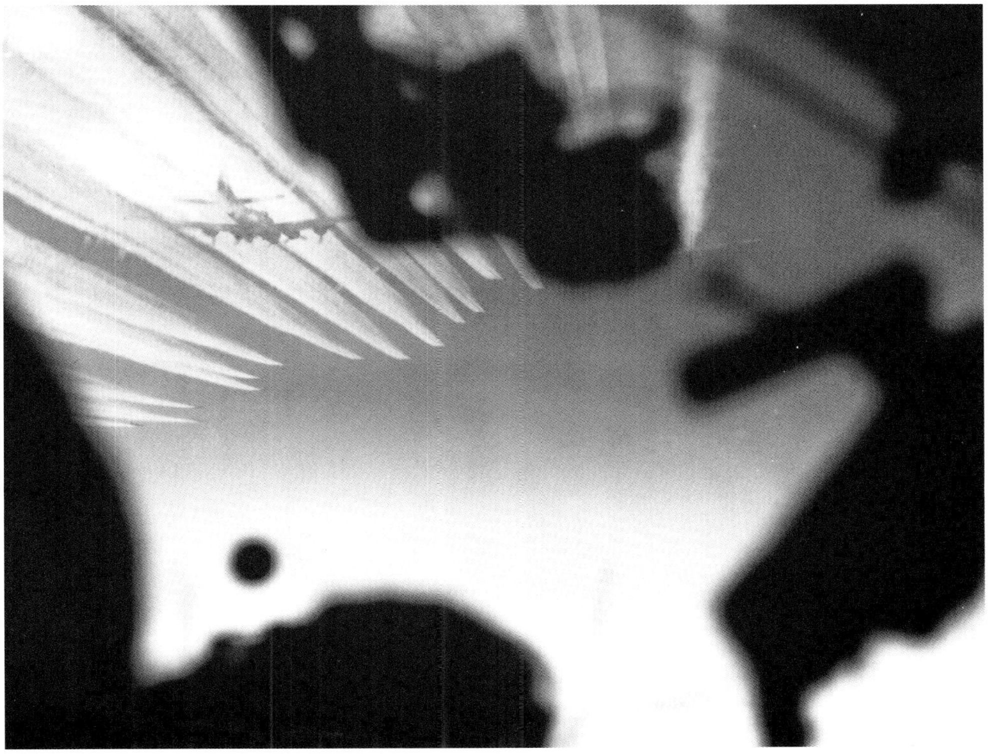

This is the view from the nose of a 452nd Bomb Group B-17. The bombardier sat in the nose and worked the nose guns when he wasn't over the bombsight. The streams of white are condensed vapor trails ("con trails") left at high altitude from the engine exhaust of the aircraft. (USAF)

A view from the left waist gun window of a B-17 of the 452nd Bomb Group shows how close the squadron formations are. (USAF)

A formation of B-17s from the 384th Bomb Group proceeds to its target regardless of German flak bursts. Once committed to the bomb run it was not possible to take evasive action from flak. (USAF)

446th Bomb Group B-24s attack a German airfield in Romilly, France. On such missions fragmentation bombs, smaller than the high explosives used on industrial targets, would be employed. The shrapnel from the fragmentation ordnance was sufficient to cripple grounded aircraft. (USAF)

A B-17 of the 381st Bomb Group over Berlin. Templehoff Airdrome is just off its right wing. (USAF)

This was part of a force of 200 B-17s of the 3rd Bomb Division attacking an aviation factory at Oberpfaffenhofen, Germany, on 18 March 1944. The nearest Fortress, at 24,000 feet, is part of the 91st Bomb Group. Seven aircraft were lost on this mission. (USAF)

Three B-17s make their bomb run over refineries at Hamburg that have already been set afire by preceding squadrons, June 1944. (USAF)

A 452nd Bomb Group B-17 unleashes its bomb load over Germany on 24 December 1944. (USAF)

Eight escorts, leaving their contrails high above, protect "Hare Power," a B-24J of the 852nd Squadron, 491st Bomb Group. Note that the Liberator's bomb bay doors are open. She was shot down on a later mission. (USAF)

A bomb dump at Framlingham, England, home of the 390th Bomb Group, is seen here. The stack in the foreground is 500 pounders, and those in the rear are 1000-pound high explosives. The fuses and tail fins will not be added until the ordnance is ready to be loaded. In the background is a B-17F of the 569th Squadron. It was lost over Germany. (USAF)

Sgt. Vernal L. Boline, tail gunner in the 389th Bomb Group, chalked a note on a 1,000-pound high explosive bomb he hoped to deliver to Hitler. (Bob Foose)

A B-17 of the 100th Bomb Group has its bomb bay doors open in preparation for release over Germany. The bombs are arrayed in two parallel racks. Note that the tail turret is firing to the right toward an approaching attacker, and the right waist gun, ball turret, and nose turret are all tracking targets on that same side. (USAF)

It's "bombs away" for these B-17s of the 306th Bomb Group unloading simultaneously deep in Germany. (USAF)

The 853rd Squadron, 491st Bomb Group targets the Vomag tank works at Plauen, Germany, just days before the German surrender. (USAF)

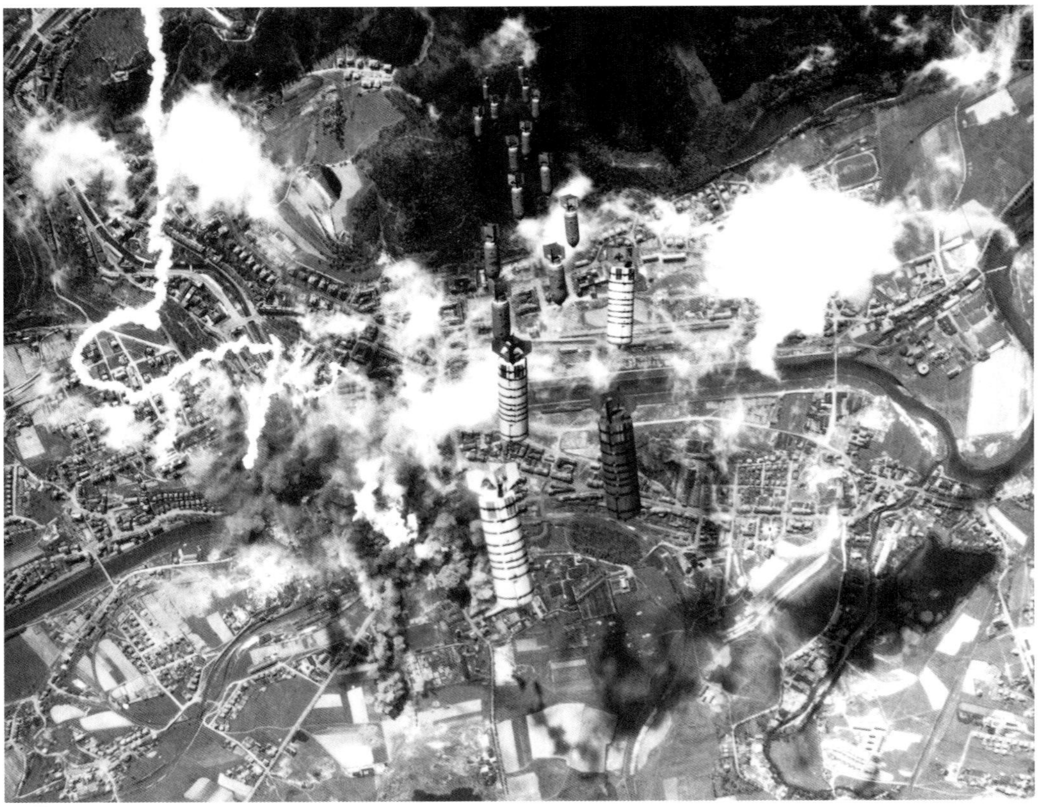

Magnesium incendiary clusters follow high explosive bombs from the bomb bay of an Eighth Air Force heavy bomber over a German city. The bundle would break and scatter small but highly inflammable units over a wide area. (USAF)

B-24 Liberators of the 93rd Bomb Group send a cascade of ncendiary bombs toward Berlin targets in March 1944. (USAF)

When called for, each group would salvo its bombs on the release of the load in the lead aircraft. Because clouds and flak could occasionally obscure the view of the lead plane, smoke marker bombs (descending smoke trail) were used as a guide for other bombardiers. These B-24s are on a m ssion over France. Note that one B-24 (center) has a smoking engine. (USAF)

Certain German targets were protected by several feet of reinforced concrete, impervious to high explosive bombs. A special rocket assisted bomb was developed that would penetrate the concrete. Carried externally under the wings of a bomber, the Disney Bomb (as it was called) would be released from 20,000 feet, and the rocket motor on the tail would actuate at 5,000 feet. It was only effective if placed with a high degree of accuracy. A pair of the bombs is being dropped here on E-boat pens at Ijmuiden, Holland. The E-boat was a fast surface attack vessel. (USAF)

After the fall of France German submarines were based on its Atlantic coast at Brest, Lorient, St. Nazaire, and LaPallaice. Sub berths, called pens, were covered with up to 15 feet of concrete, and were never seriously damaged by conventional bombing, although the support facilities and the towns around these sub bases suffered heavily. Eighth Air Force expended many missions and many lives against these targets. Here is a view of the entrance to one of the heavily constructed sub pens at Lorient. (USAF)

This B-24J was pathfinder (or lead aircraft) for the 93rd Bomb Group. In place of the belly ball turret it carried an H2S radar housed in the bulbous radome. The lead aircraft bombed through overcast, aiming with its radar, and other Liberators salvoed on sighting its drop. The pathfinders often used smoke marker bombs. (USAF)

A synthetic oil plant at Bohlen, Germany, is under attack by the Eighth Air Force. In what appears here as a transparent effort, the Germans light smoke pots to hide this important industrial facility. Although smoke was not an uncommon defense tactic, radar equipped pathfinders were immune to smoke screens. (USAF)

P-51 Mustangs leave their comforting contrails above a B-17 of the 100th Bomb Group. The men of the Eighth Air Force called the fighters "little friends," and the fighter pilots referred to the heavy bombers as "big friends." The fighter pilots offered protection, and the big bombers often helped the fighters navigate back to England. (USAF)

Some of the "little friends" line up for the takeoff queue at Halesworth, England. The fighters took to the air in pairs. These are Republic P-47s of the 56th Fighter Group. (Bob Foose)

B-24s of the 493rd Bomb Group, with engines turning, taxi into the takeoff queue at Little Walden, England. (Bob Foose)

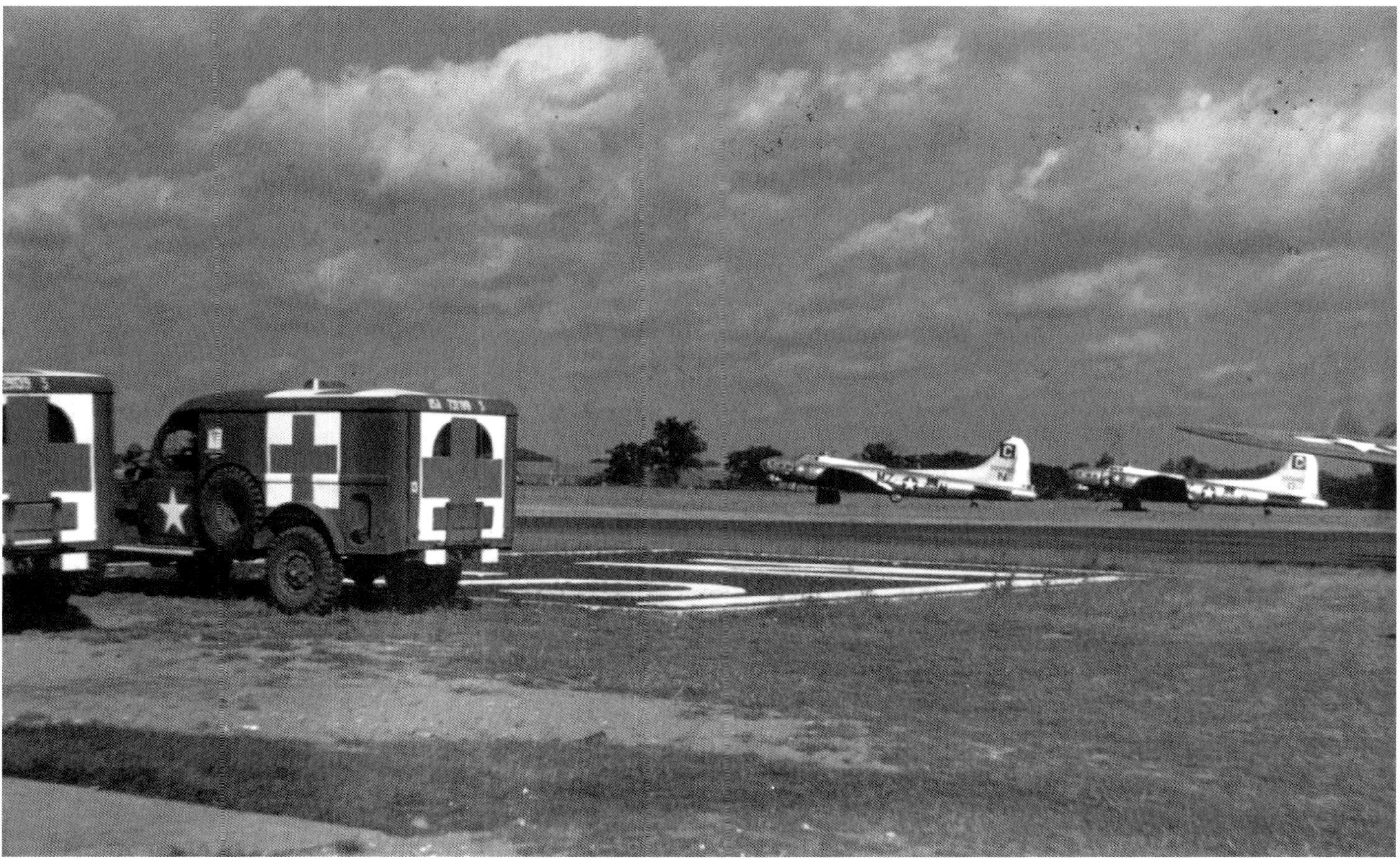

B-17s of the 96th Bomb Group prepare for takeoff at Snetterton Heath England. The ambulances (foreground) and crash trucks were always present at the start and end of each mission. (Bob Foose)

With hundreds of aircraft taking off from eastern England at approximately the same time, all needing to organize into units and assemble with their squadron or group, "form-up" ships were employed. This one was with the 93rd Bomb Group. (USAF)

Another "form-up" ship was the shark mouthed, polka dot painted B-24 served on assembly duty with the 458th Bomb group. It also bore the name, "Spotted Ass Ape." These old timers carried no guns, and would return to base after the formations were gathered and on their way. (USAF)

This garishly designed old B-24D served as an assembly ship for the 2nd Bomb Division of the Eighth Air Force in 1944. She is shown here in the markings of the 392nd Bomb Group at Wendling, England. (USAF)

Fortress Leaving Calais

They say there's a Fortress leaving Calais,
Bound for old Limey Shore.
It's heavily laden with petrified men,
And stiffs who are laid on the floor.
Many a Focke-Wulf made many a pass,
And many a Messerschmitt too.
They shot off our bollicks,
Shot up our hydraulics,
But cheer up, my lads,
Bless 'em all!

Chorus:
Bless 'em all, bless 'em all,
The long and the short and the tall.
Bless all the blondies and all the brunettes,
Each airman is happy to take what he gets.
So we're giving the eye to 'em all,
To those who attract and appall,
Each Sally and Suzie,
You can't be too choosy.
So cheer up, my lads,
Bless 'em all!

With six QDM's and some bloody good luck,
We made the limey Shore.
The cloud was eleven-tenths,
Right on the deck,
And tried bloody hard to be more.
We dug up a windmill and six thatched-roof shacks,
When they traced us back to landfall.
Now there'll be no promotion,
This side of the ocean,
So cheer up, my lads,
Bless 'em all!

Unknown Eighth Air Force crews in England adapted this story of a B-17 mission to France. It derived from an old British barracks ballad, "Troopship Leaving Bombay," and was sung to the tune of the ever popular, "Bless 'em all."

B-17s of the 569th Squadron, 490th Bomb Group return to Framlingham, England. They always approached the base in a proud tactical formation, despite some missing aircraft, and peeled off one-by-one for a 360-degree turn before landing. (Bob Foose)

Liberators of the 93rd Bomb Group let down in formation near their base at Hardwick, England. (USAF)

"The Shark," a B-24H of the 44th Bomb Group's 67th Squadron, turns on base leg for its field at Shipdham, England. (USAF)

Liberator Blues

Now, the Liberator's a very fine airplane
Constructed of rivets and tin,
With a speed of over 200-
The ship with the head wind built in.

Yes, the Lib is a very fine airplane,
Constructed of paper and wood.
It's O.K. for luggin' whiskey,
But for combat it's no God damn good.

Oh, why did I join the Air Force?
Mother, dear mother, knew best.
Here I lie 'neath the wreckage,
Liberator all over my chest.

Now if you should go on a mission,
With plenty of money to burn,
Any old crew chief will give you
A bet that you'll never return.

And if you should run into trouble,
And don't know which way to turn,
Just reach up on the panel, my lad.
Push the button marked, "Spin, Crash, and Burn!"

The author of this bit of black humor is unknown, but it may have been a B-17 pilot. However, the men who flew the B-24 swore by them.

Jettisonable fuel tanks to augment the range of fighters came on the scene in late 1943. The early ones were ungainly 200-gallon ferry tanks that caused flight stability problems when only half full. Disposable lightweight tanks of 75 gallons and then 108 gallons became available early in 1944. Seen here is a stack of the 108s at Halesworth, England. (USAF)

A pair of 108-gallon drop tanks mounted under the wing of a 357th Fighter Group P-51D. They would be jettisoned when empty in favor of internal storage tanks, or at the first encounter with enemy aircraft. (Lambert)

2

The Aircraft

The bomber advocates of the U.S. Army Air Force were planning the Boeing B-17 Flying Fortress as early as 1935. When World War II finally engulfed the U.S., B-17s immediately saw action in the Pacific. Production of the B-17E was well underway, but early combat lessons caused modifications. The "F" variant was the first Fortress that saw wartime mass production. At war's end 12,726 B-17s had been produced.

The B-17 had four Wright Cyclone engines, cruised at 160 mph, was 74 feet in length, and had a wingspan of 103 feet, 9 inches. The F model had six .50 caliber machine guns in power turrets, and five or six flexible guns at various locations. Starting with the "G" model, a chin turret of twin-.50s was added. The B-17F and G had a bomb capacity of 8,000 pounds.

Consolidated Aircraft's experimental version of a heavy bomber arrived on the scene in 1939, and a desperate need saw it going into production in January 1942. The first combat model was the B-24D Liberator. By the end of World War II 18,188 Liberators had been built, and were operated in every theatre of war by the AAF and several Allies. The Lib was built in variants up to the "M" Model, and ultimately carried eight .50 caliber machine guns in power turrets and two more on flexible mounts. The AAF versions had a 66-foot length and a 110-foot wingspan. The airfoil, of radical design, seemed too narrow to sustain the boxy bomber. The "Davis Wing," named after its designer, was an experiment to provide greater lift. Equipped with four Pratt & Whitney engines, the B-24 had somewhat greater speed, range, and bomb load than the B-17. It cruised at near 190 mph.

Fortress and Liberator crews swore by their various ships, but the Eighth Air Force command favored the B-17 for survivability, and converted several groups from the B-24 to the B-17. At the end of the war in Europe the Eighth mustered 27 groups of B-17s and 13 of B-24s.

The evolution of the Eighth Fighter Command lagged the operations of the Bomber Command because of the mistaken notion that the heavily armed bombers could take care of themselves. The Luftwaffe proved that wrong.

The 4th Fighter Group began its service in England with borrowed, short-range, RAF Spitfires. Quantities of U.S. produced fighters were not received in England until the spring of 1943, when Republic P-47 Thunderbolts arrived. A sturdy aircraft that could hold its own with the Luftwaffe, early P-47Ds also lacked the range for deep escort. In due course, modified versions of the P-47 and disposable wing tanks made the Thunderbolt a long-range fighter.

A few Lockheed P-38 Lightnings had arrived in England late in 1942. They had a range of approximately 500 miles, but were plagued by a series of mechanical problems that limited their capability, and caused the loss of several pilots. The early units of P-38s were transferred to North Africa, and the remainder proved their worth after various modifications had resolved the mechanical bugs.

The fighter that eventually solved the long-range escort dilemma was the North American P-51 Mustang. Designed as a low-level attack aircraft, the American airframe wed to the British Rolls Royce Merlin engine (produced by Packard) turned it into the consummate long-range escort. Ultimately all Eighth Fighter Command groups but one would convert to the P-51.

The early Fortress was a graceful beauty. B-17Fs of the 303rd Bomb Group are attacking German airdromes at Amiens/Glisy in France in 1943. Note the flak bursts within the formation. The Big Friends had to defend themselves during these early missions. Allied fighters could only escort them a short distance into France, and then meet them at the same point on the return. (USAF)

This is a late model B-17F, distinguished by the so-called "chin" turret under the nose. German fighters soon learned that attacking in a head-on pass was less dangerous than any other approach; hence, the addition of a pair of .50s in a power turret. This ship is "Bacta-th' Sac," No. 42-3540 of the 535th Squadron, 381st Bomb Group. It was lost to German fighters on 1 December 1943 over Leverkusen, Germany. (USAF)

The Flying Fortress was an attractive aircraft in flight or on the ground. This 388th Bomb Group Model G was a veteran of many missions, as shown by the bombs marked on the nose. Here it is warming up for one more sortie from Knettishall, England. (USAF)

The late G Model B-17s arrived in natural metal finish (NMF) from factories in the U.S. Crews sometimes referred to the unpainted Forts and Libs as "naked." Serial No. 43-37520 (foreground) was one of five 560th Squadron, 388th Bomb Group Forts lost over Merseburg, Germany, on 28 September 1944. (USAF)

The Liberator's great slab side seemed to offer an irresistible canvas for nose artists. "Poop Deck Pappy" was an H model, No. 42-7521, which served with the 577th Squadron, 392nd Bomb Group. She was wrecked in a crash landing at Shipdam, England, on 16 November 1944. (USAF)

Above: The contrast between the bulky fuselage and the narrow Davis wing is apparent in this view of 409th Squadron, 93rd Bomb Group Libs. The early model B-24Hs came in camouflage paint. Later versions from Ford, Willow Run, were in natural metal finish (NMF). The Liberator in the foreground was lost over Tours airdromes, France, on 5 February 1944. (USAF)

Right: "Tailwind," a B-24H (No. 41-29368) of the 789th Squadron, 467th Bomb Group was lost over Munich on 11 July 1944. The pilot, 1st Lt. James Underwood, and two other crewmembers were killed, and seven became prisoners of war (POWs). (Ed Kueppers)

B-24s of the 446th Bomb Group attack chemical works at Ludwigshafen, Germany, on 31 July 1944. The 2nd Air Division lost six aircraft on this mission. Note the black flak bursts from AA fire coming through the layer of clouds. En route to a target visible flak barrages could sometimes be avoided. But once the bombing run had begun no evasive action was possible. (USAF)

The first U.S fighter unit in the Eighth Air Force was the 4th Fighter Group, and was formed around the men and aircraft of the RAF Eagle Squadrons—Americans who had volunteered to fight for Britain before 7 December 1941. This is a Supermarine Spitfire, one of the breed that saved England during the German aerial Blitz of 1940-41. The Spit's short range soon left it in the wake of the strategic air war. (Garry Fry)

The first American made fighters to join the 8th Fighter Command in any numbers were Republic Thunderbolts. This P-47D-RE served with the 61st Squadron, 56th Fighter Group. The earliest Thunderbolts were called "Razorbacks." This one has a new drop tank installed under the belly, and was piloted by 1st Lt. Dick H. Mudge, Jr. Both plane and pilot were later downed, Mudge becoming a POW. (Bob Dorr)

Republic delivered many variants of the P-47 over the course of the war. Here is a shot of the takeoff of a pair of D models. The older Razorback is ahead of a new bubble canopy version. Both are from the 56th Fighter Group. (Bob Foose)

The Lockheed P-38 Lightning arrived late in 1942 with units destined for North Africa. They exhibited several mechanical problems that were addressed by the time the 55th Fighter Group was assigned to the Eighth Air Force. The P-38 never quite lived up to its "long-range" press notices, and all three P-38 groups in the Eighth were eventually converted to P-51s. (USAF)

The incomparable North American Mustang began escort service with the Eighth Air Force at the end of 1943. This is an early version, a P-51B-10NA, named "Impatient Virgin." It served with the 367th Squadron, 361st Fighter Group. (Lambert)

The airdrome at Bodney, England, was home to the 352nd Fighter Group. Here is a collection of various 352nd Mustang models and paint schemes. The white and black stripes around the center fuselage were special D-Day markings. (Lambert)

B-24s of the 458th Bomb Group under escort by P-51 Mustangs of the 352nd Fighter Group. Scenes such as this were a comfort to both the Big Friends and Little Friends alike. If German aircraft appeared they were called "Bandits." (USAF)

A variant of the Lockheed P-38, the F-5, served as the eyes of the Eighth Air Force with the 7th Photo Reconnaissance Group. (Bob Foose)

The 7th Photo Recon Group also employed the British-built deHaviland Mosquito, a twin-engined gazelle. (USAF)

3

The Crews

It took nine or ten to man a four-engined B-17 or a B-24. The crew generally consisted of a pilot who was aircraft commander, a co-pilot, bombardier, navigator (all officers), and an enlisted crew of six: engineer, radioman, and gunners. The lone pilot served all these roles in a fighter aircraft.

The bombers flew in tight squadron/group formations so that their many defensive machine guns could provide mutual support. A German fighter generally had to brave the fire of the formation. When an attacker smoked or burned it was often claimed by several gunners from different ships, resulting in multiple claims for a single kill.

Virtually all bombing missions flew at high altitude, thus requiring warm weather clothing. Still, that was not always sufficient to ward off the cold. In the early stages of the Eighth Air Force campaign frostbite was not an infrequent problem above 20,000 feet, where winter temperatures could reach minus 60 degrees. It was not until 1943 that electrically heated flying suits became available.

Flights above 12,000 feet also required oxygen. Thus, both fighter and bomber crews were wired to heat, oxygen, and radio. In addition they wore the so-called "Mae West" inflatable life jacket and a parachute harness. Bomber crews had to attach chest parachute packs in case of an emergency. The fighter pilot had a seat pack that was always attached to his parachute harness. As the air war marched to its grim conclusion flak jackets and helmets became available for the bomber crews.

Both bombers and fighters had non-flying crewmembers: the personnel who serviced their aircraft. These unsung heroes were devoted to their aircraft and crews, and were determined that "their ship" would not fail or abort because of any mechanical flaw. They watched the mission's departure, sweated out the long return, then frequently worked through the night repairing battle damage or servicing their charges.

Initially the bomber crews had a quota of 25 combat missions. Many never got there, and the chances were statistically against completion of the 25 goal in late 1943. But as long-range fighters began to turn the war in favor of the Eighth Air Force the quota was raised to 30, and then 35 missions. Still, the losses in aggregate were staggering.

In this chapter we will show a representative few of the men who flew and serviced the aircraft of the Eighth Air Force. Their missions depended on teamwork, courage under fire, and the grit to keep facing the terror again and again.

A B-24 crewman in cold weather gear. Note the sheepskin flying boots The electric heating cord entered at the jacket pocket. The line from the helmet connected him to the intercom on the bomber, and the hose from the mask went to an oxygen bottle. (USAF)

A B-24 navigator considers his various equipment and impedimenta. (Bob Foose)

A pair of buddies, these are the waist gunners in a 453rd Bomb Group B-24. They worked back to back as they operated their single .50 caliber machine guns. (Bob Foose)

One of the two waist gunners of a B-17. He fired a single flexible .50 caliber machine gun. The ammo belt came from boxes mounted to the left of the gun. Note that the gunner's parachute pack is on the floor held by a tether so that it could be retrieved quickly. (USAF)

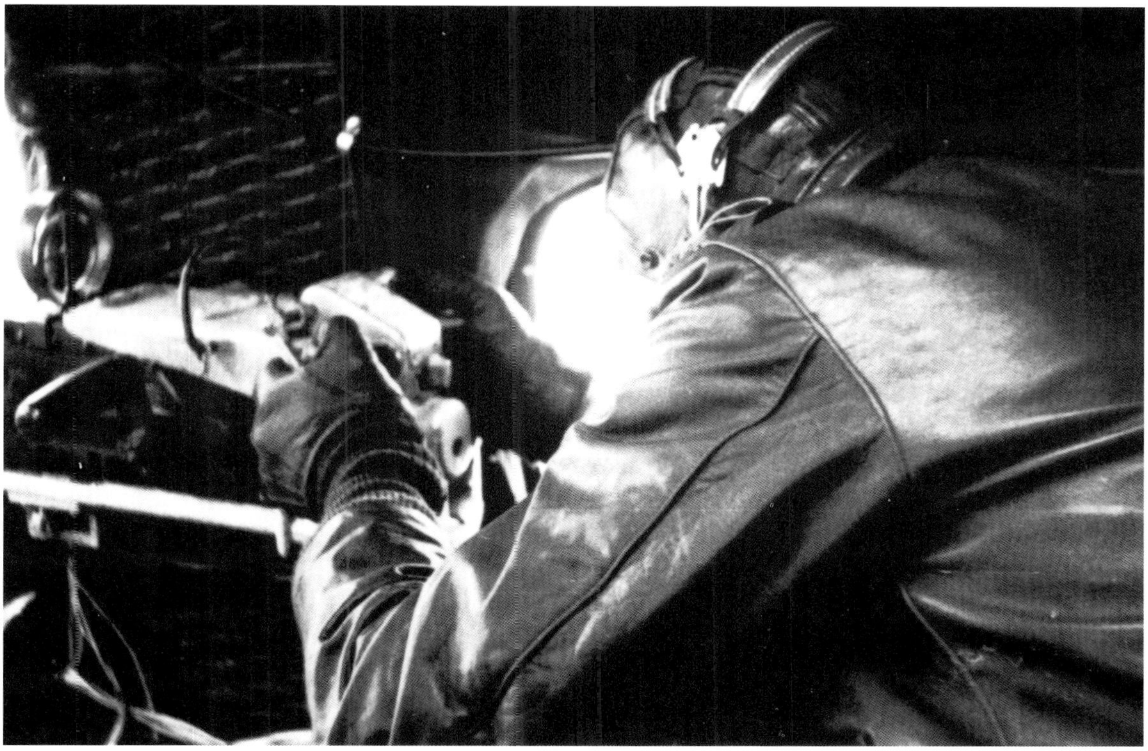

A navigator or bombardier operating a single, flexible machine gun installed in the nose cheek of a B-17. (USAF)

This 91st Bomb Group enlisted crew chief was also top turret gunner. The Fortress power turret, with twin .50s, was just aft of the flight deck. (Bob Foose)

The view from the caboose, the tail power turret of a B-24 Liberator. (Bob Foose)

A picture of the tail turret of the B-17 "Mary Lou," 323rd Squadron, 91st Bomb Group (Bob Foose)

One had to be small and devoid of any claustrophobic tendencies to be a ball turret gunner. Some of the enlisted crew discuss the adventure of riding the ball turret of this 486th Bomb group B-17. The gunner could not fit in the power turret with the twin .50s and ammo while wearing a parachute. If ordered to bail out he had to exit the turret into the aircraft, retrieve and hook up his chute, then depart through the bomb bay or a side hatch. (USAF)

A B-17 ball turret gunner's view forward past the open bomb bay doors. The target below was the Merseburg/Leuna oil complex. (USAF)

Crews were awakened in the early morning dark, had breakfast, went to a briefing, donned their flight gear, and prepared for takeoff at sunrise. Before dawn officers from the 452nd Bomb Group study a route map for a deep penetration mission to Ruhland, Germany. The 3rd Air Division would continue on to airfields in western Russia, near Kiev. (USAF)

This 10-man crew of the 562nd Squadron, 388th Bomb Group, is outfitted and ready for a mission. They are: (l. to r.) top row: Lts. Clyde Richardson, Francis Hennessey (Pilot), Ed Neft, and Sidney Mink. Lower (l. to r.): enlisted crew: John Lynch, James Mack, Lewis Pursley, Howard Weeks, John McCullough, and Marcus Moore. They all survived the war, but "Captain Joe" did not. It was shot down over Frankfurt, Germany, with another crew on 20 March 1944. (USAF)

Lt. Wiley's 92nd Bomb Group crew pose with the B-17 "Mag the Hag." Crew and aircraft survived the war. (USAF)

The ground crews of a B-24 outfit watch as their aircraft depart on a mission. They will "sweat it out" until the planes return. (USAF)

"Freckles," a B-17 from the 601st Squadron, 401st Bomb Group, undergoes maintenance by ground crews at Deenethorpe. The English weather was not always this cooperative. She was lost on 31 July 1944. (Bob Foose)

The crew of B-17G "Lady Geraldine" returns from a mission, and begin to shed their flight gear. This ship served with the 418th Squadron, 100th Bomb Group. Round trips into Germany could involve six to nine hours of flying. (Bob Foose)

"Thru Hel'en Hiwater" is back to Thorpe Abbots, England, from a mission, and its crew climbs into a truck for transport to debriefing. The B-17G (No. 42-39875) was lost on 10 January 1945 over Hamm, Germany, with the Larson crew of the 358th Squadron, 303rd Bomb Group. Four were killed, and six were POWs. (USAF)

The war lover. Lt. Col. Manny Klette flew 91 combat missions with the 306th and 91st Bomb Groups. In September 1943 he returned his damaged plane, "Connecticut Yankee," to England short of fuel and survived a crash landing. Despite this he volunteered again and again to continue flying missions. Here he is shown near the end of the war in the B-17G, "Klette's Wild Hares." (USAF)

Col. Hubert Zemke (above) and Lt. Col. Francis Gabreski (right) were aces of the 56th Fighter Group. Zemke scored 17 victories over the Luftwaffe, transferred to the 479th Fighter Group, and became a POW. Gabreski was the leading U.S. ace in Europe, with 28 kills in 153 missions. He also stretched his luck too far and became a POW when forced to crash land in Germany. (USAF)

A deadly duo from the 4th Fighter Group, Capt. John Godfrey (left) and Capt. Don Gentile, frequently flew with each other, scoring a combined 38 aerial victories. On his second combat tour, Godfrey was shot down and made a prisoner while airdrome strafing. They flew the Spitfire, P-47, and P-51. The wings on their right breast reflect that both had previously served with the RAF. (USAF)

Lt. Warren Wesson of the 82nd Squadron, 78th Fighter Group watches as his crew chief, Tech Sgt. Clarence Koskela, paints another victory flag on the P-47D. Wesson, like many fighter pilots, carried the name of his ground crew on his aircraft. "Jeanie" is Wesson's wife. The "V.O.S." stands for victory over separat on. (USAF)

Capt. Jack Ilfrey carries his combat score on the nose of his P-38J of the 79th Squadron, 20th Fighter Group. He had served a previous combat tour in North Africa and volunteered for a second tour. His total record was 7 1/2 aerial victories. His P-38 also shows symbols for a couple of Nazi locomotives bagged while strafing. (Lambert)

1st Lt. Urban Drew, 375th Squadron, 361st Fighter Group, is congratulated by his crew chief after returning from a mission in which he downed a pair of German Me 262 jets. The 361st began its combat duty with the P-47, but transitioned to the P-51. (Lambert)

Fighter pilots from the Mustang equipped 505th Squadron, 339th Fighter Group: (l. to r.) 1st Lt. Oscar Biggs, Capt. Jim Starnes, and Capt. George Rich. (Lambert)

With skill, teamwork, and a lot of luck, some crews survived the ordeal. The O'Brien crew of the 489th Bomb Group stand next to their B-24H "Pin Up Girl." The panel beneath the pilot's window, with mission symbols, was armor plate added in the field. (M.A. O'Brien)

"Rhapsody in Red," a B-17G of the 91st Bomb Group, served several crews well. She survived the war after 95 missions. Seen here is the Tom Martin crew of the 324th Squadron. (USAF)

4

The Opposition

The German military had planned a modern air force long before the start of World War II. They tested both their theories and equipment in Spain in the mid-1930s, and so had a considerable head start on Allied nations influenced by anti-military factions. As a consequence, the Luftwaffe was both numerically and technically superior to the air arms of Europe and the U.S. in 1939. Their assault on England in 1940 almost succeeded in defeating the British. It was only through the courage of a few RAF fighter pilots, and the tactical interference of Hitler, that Great Britain survived.

Thus, in August 1942, when the U.S. Eighth Air Force began its campaign of daylight precision bombing of northern European targets, the relative handful of B-17s constituted mere pin pricks. The Luftwaffe reaction was tepid regarding attacks on Northern France and the Low Countries. Over Atlantic Coast submarine bases the opposition became more intense. It was not until mid-1943, when air raids into Germany began, that the Luftwaffe took an unacceptable toll of attacking bombers, and the deeper the penetration into Germany, the stronger the opposition and the steeper the price. The numbers of B-17s being put over Germany were increasing, as was the loss ratio.

With the arrival of long-range escorts for the B-17s and B-24s early in 1944, the loss ratio became more bearable for the Eighth Air Force. Yet, despite attacks on German airfields and aircraft production facilities, the Luftwaffe continued a ferocious resistance to both night and day bombing. To the consternation of Allied air leaders, the German fighter defense seemed not to slacken despite the claims for scores of German interceptors being destroyed in aerial combat. In fact, due to the dispersal of aircraft manufacturing and airfields, the German fighter supply actually increased sharply in the first six months of 1944. At this stage of the war it was only the demands of a three front war that kept the Luftwaffe from asserting dominance over the Allied bomber fleets.

German anti-aircraft artillery defenses likewise increased, as the air war grew more intense. The number of heavy artillery pieces in German flak units on all fronts in 1942 was some 4,700 guns. By August 1944 almost 11,000 heavy AA guns were protecting the Reich, while thousands more 20 and 37 mm cannons made airfield strafing a hazardous venture.

These defenses extracted a terrible toll of Allied aircraft. Still, it was not enough to save Germany. The 1944 strategy to attack airfields, and the constant chipping away at its force of veteran airmen spelled doom for the Luftwaffe and Germany. It was a war of attrition that Germany could not win, and one that could not be lost by the Allies given America's manpower and industrial potential.

One of the best artillery pieces of World War II was the German 88mm cannon, also employed as its primary AA gun. This battery, set into a coastal emplacement, guarded Hitler's Atlantic Wall in France. Other batteries were arrayed in belts around cities and industrial targets. The 88 could fire to 35,000 feet, with the shells set to explode at a preset altitude. The Germans also employed 105 and 128mm cannons. The rings painted on the barrel of the near gun denote the batteries' claim for Allied bombers downed. (Bob Foose)

Some AA guns were set on railroad cars, and were moved about to confuse Allied intelligence as to location. At high altitude a heavy caliber AA round exploding within 30 yards could knock out a bomber. Shrapnel from a burst could inflict damage up to 200 yards. (Bob Foose)

German heavy AA worked with radar, searchlights, and sound locators (shown here) to predict the path of approaching bomber formations. The flak batteries would then fire a box barrage in the path of the raiders. (Bob Foose)

To protect against aircraft flying at lower altitudes, the Germans employed thousands of 20 and 37mm cannons. The quad unit shown here is mounted on a rooftop. The most modern of the light AA could fire at a rate of 500 rounds per minute. (Bob Foose)

Flak towers such as this one were built to guard airdromes. They could pepper strafing aircraft with automatic weapons fire. This one, seen through a gun camera lens, is engaged in a duel with a strafing P-47. (USAF)

The Messerschmitt Bf 109 was the most heavily produced fighter aircraft of the '30 and '40s – some 30,000 in many variants. It served in the Spanish Civil War, on every World War II battlefront, flew with the air arms of several German allies, and was built on license in Spain and Switzerland. Although it had some mean tendencies on takeoff and landing, it took a heavy toll of bombers with its mix of machine guns and cannons. (Bob Foose)

The Focke-Wulf 190 was the Luftwaffe's best single-engine fighter, and a match for the best Allied fighters. Built in many variants, it is curious that it was not produced in favor of later versions of the Me. 109, which were outclassed by 1944. The 190 had a mix of machine guns and cannons that were punishing in bomber attacks. It was an outstanding performer at high altitudes. (Lambert)

Designed as a long-range escort, the Messerschmitt Bf 110 was outclassed by every British single-engine fighter, and was soon relegated to other roles, such as army support and night fighting. It was also employed against unescorted U.S. daylight raiders. Later versions had four cannons of 20 and 30mm caliber that were lethal against bombers. (Bob Foose)

As the Eighth Fighter Command began hunting tactics against the Luftwaffe German airdromes became unsafe. Fighters like these FW 190s were secreted under camouflage near forests. Note the use of two under-wing disposable fuel tanks. (Lambert)

A radical design by Messerschmitt was the Me. 163, a rocket propelled aircraft of high performance but low endurance. The "Komet" flew at just under 600 miles per hour, but only had enough fuel for a few minutes of flight. 370 were built and had no impact on the bombing campaign. (Foose)

The world's first operational jet fighter was the Messerschmitt 262. Its speed of 540 miles per hour made it faster than any Allied fighter. Still, several were shot down near landing grounds. It first became operational in mid-1944, and might have made a difference in German air defense if Hitler had not dabbled in its production. It was a formidable aircraft, and potentially the greatest fighter of the war. But the Fürher insisted on bomber and ground attack versions to the detriment of German air defense. Just over 1,400 of all types were produced. (Bob Foose)

Despite the Allies' Combined Bombing Offensive, German aircraft production increased until near the end of 1944. Here is the production line for Me 110s at Gotha, Germany. (Bob Foose)

The Messerschmitt works attempted successors to the Me 110 ending with the Me 410. It was used primarily as a night fighter, and to attack Eighth Air Force bombers when unescorted. It mounted cannons or several machine guns, and by 1944 was fitted with rockets. Units so equipped would fly next to the bomber stream, out of range of their .50 cal. machine guns, and lob rockets into the packed formations. (Bob Foose)

An Me 410 thunders through a formation of the 388th Bomb Group near Brux, Germany, passing just off the wing of "Lady Godiva." (USAF)

An Me 410 makes a tail attack on a formation of 100th Bomb Group B-17s. The action occurred during a 1943 mission to Schweinfurt, Germany. (USAF)

"Our Gal Sal," a B-24 of the 701st Squadron, 445th Bomb Group, crash-landed on the Continent, and is being inspected by Luftwaffe personnel. (Ed Kueppers)

This B-17F, No. 42-3186 of Lt. Coleman Goldstein, was shot down in the Bordeaux region of France on 31 December 1943. Six of the 407th Squadron, 92nd Bomb Group crewmembers evaded capture, but four became prisoners. (USAF)

"Miss Ouachita" was one of 41 bombers downed over Central Germany on 22 February 1944. German fighter pilot Lt. Col. Heinz Baer was the victor over this B-17F, No. 42-3040 from the 323rd Squadron, 91st Bomb Group. Baer had over 200 kills against Allied aircraft, including 21 four-engined types. (USAF)

Among Luftwaffe fighter pilots, Maj. George-Peter Eder was the expert at "killing" four-engined American bombers. He was credited with downing 36 Liberators and Fortresses. Eder preferred to attack head-on where the closing speed was near 600 mph, thus minimizing the potential for damage from the combined defensive fire of bomber formations. Still, he was shot down or obliged to crash land 17 times, nine times as a result of defensive fire from Eighth Air Force bombers. His mounts were the FW 190 and, late in the war, the Me. 262 jet fighter. His overall score of victories was 78. Incredibly, he survived the war. (Bob Foose)

Col. Gustav Roedel was another German pilot who specialized in destroying B-17s and B-24s, with 12 such kills. Of his 98 confirmed victories all but one was on the Western Front. Roedel flew 1,000 combat missions and survived the war. (Bob Foose)

A German Me.262 jet fighter was caught at low altitude as it let down for its home base on 15 February 1945. This gun camera shot was made by lst Lt. Dudley Moss, 55th Fighter group. (Lambert)

Gen. Doolittle's directive to "seek and destroy" the Luftwaffe in the air or on the ground is carried out by this Eighth Air Force fighter pilot. His gun camera records the attack as .50 cal. rounds pour d a group of parked Me 110s. Note the incredibly low level. (USAF)

5

Casualties and Near Misses

The toll of human life that resulted from World War II is almost beyond reckoning. It is estimated that there were over 48 million military and civilian deaths as a result of the global conflict. The United States suffered a relatively small percentage of the deaths thanks to the isolation offered by its two ocean barriers. Still, the American Battle Monuments Commission records 405,399 as dead or missing. Of the numbered units in each of the various U.S. military branches, the Eighth Air Force suffered the highest casualties: 26,000 were killed in action, and another 28,000 were shot down and made prisoners of war. Thousands more were wounded.

Enemy action was largely responsible for the deaths. However, operational losses were ever present. The takeoff and assembly dangers were unimaginable when compared to the precise air traffic control mechanisms of today. With ground fog and cloud cover consistent elements in England, aircraft collisions occurred even while taxiing.

As the swarms of aircraft climbed to altitude from scores of airfields they frequently had to lift through low hanging overcast, executing ascending racetrack patterns while group formations assembled. There were generally twelve bombers to a squadron, and four squadrons to a group. Hundreds of aircraft from airfields in close proximity were simultaneously maneuvering to locate their units as they climbed to altitude. The potential for disaster was manifest. Pilots flying on instruments through murky weather reported seeing ghostly shadows passing close by, the bare outlines of other aircraft groping toward clear sky.

There were also instances of planes losing power on takeoff and coming back to earth in flaming explosions. In every such case the bombers and fighters were fully loaded with fuel and, in the case of the bombers, with a deadly cargo of explosives.

Once over Occupied Europe flight crews ran the gauntlet of enemy flak and fighters. Neither could be readily avoided by the large bomber formations—merely endured. While intelligence attempted to route bombing missions around known flak belts, the Germans would frequently move these batteries, posing unavoidable threats.

Aircraft damaged by enemy action could occasionally limp back to England; this did not assure the survival of bomber and fighter crews. The warbirds were often crippled too badly for a routine landing. As damaged bombers approached their bases, flares were fired from those with wounded aboard. It was not an uncommon sight.

Crash landings occurred all over Southern England. Some ditched in the cold North Sea, where survival depended on the prompt action of RAF rescue boats. When aircraft were seriously damaged far from England their crews were obliged to parachute or face a crash landing. Thousands of aircrew members ended up in German prisoner of war (POW) camps. A few lucky crews, knowing they could not reach England, chose to go down in neutral Sweden or Switzerland. There they were interred for the rest of the war, but under more tolerable conditions than existed in Germany.

The peril of flying missions over German occupied territory were so great that those crewmembers reaching the coveted quota of complete missions (25, 30, or 35) received certificates of membership in the Lucky Bastard Club.

It was only the third daylight raid staged by the Eighth Air Force's heavy bombers, but it gave a preview of things to come. A formation of 12 B-17s attacked a shipyard in Rotterdam, Holland. "Johnny Reb," of the 97th Bomb group, lagged behind the others, was set upon by FW 190 fighters, and received a cannon shell hit through the right windscreen. It killed the copilot, 2nd Lt. Donald Walters, wrecked the cockpit, blew out the top turret, and burned the pilot, 2nd Lt. Richard F. Sparks. Several other crewmembers were wounded. The bombardier, 2nd Lt. E.T. Sconiers, took over the controls and nursed the Fortress back to England for a belly landing. (USAF)

On 30 July 1943 some 130 B-17s from six groups were assigned to bomb the Fiesler aircraft plant at Kassel, Germany. Flak and fighter attacks were intense, and six Forts were downed. This is the crash scene of "Wing and a Prayer," of the 388th Bomb Group. AA hits knocked out the No. 1 and 3 engines and damaged the hydraulics for the bomb bay doors before the target was reached. Unable to stay in formation, Bombardier Lt. David Adams hand cranked the doors open and jettisoned the bombs one at a time with a screwdriver. German fighters knocked out the other two engines, and all crewmembers parachuted through the open bomb bay. (Bob Foose)

Lt. Karl R. Alexander, navigator on "Wing and a Prayer," broke an ankle when he landed, and was helped to medical assistance by German farmers. The entire crew spent the next two years in prison camps. (Bob Foose)

Many aircraft damaged in battle over Germany that could not make it back to England elected to go down in Switzerland. During the Stuttgart raid of 9 June 1943 the 100th Bomb Group's B-17F "Raunchy" bellied onto Lake Constance. It is shown here being removed from the water many months later. The crew was interned except for the tail gunner, Joe Malone, who died. (Bob Foose)

One of the Schweinfurt raiders of 10 October 1943, when 60 B-17s were shot down. German soldiers seem to be attempting to extricate the tail gunner. This was an F model from the 306th Bomb Group. The group lost 10 of 23 aircraft dispatched. (Bob Foose)

On 14 October 1943, in the aftermath of the deadly Schweinfurt mission, a B-17F of the 364th Squadron, 305th Bomb Group was damaged. Two crewmembers bailed out, but with wounded aboard the pilot, Lt. Edward Dinehard, elected to try for a crash landing. He came to ground in the Reinach, Switzerland, area, and the crew was interned. (Bob Foose)

Navigator Lt. Donald T. Rowley died of his wounds in a Swiss hospital, shown here being buried with full military honors. The Swiss permitted his interned comrades of the 364th to act as pallbearers. (Bob Foose)

A captive of the Luftwaffe. This B-17F of the 303rd Bomb Group crash-landed in Occupied France after being damaged near Rouen on 12 December 1942. The pilot, 1st Lt. Paul Flickenger, was taken prisoner, but several of the crewmembers evaded capture and, with the help of the French underground, returned to England. However, the Fortress was repainted in Luftwaffe markings and test flown. (Bob Foose)

On 20 June 1944 over 1,600 Eighth Air Force heavy bombers attacked targets from Pas de Calais to Poland. Fifty were lost to various causes, including this B-24H of the 389th Bomb Group. She crash-landed, and the crew were made POWs. The Lib was repaired and evaluated by the Luftwaffe. (Bob Foose)

This P-47D of the 358th Squadron, 355th Fighter Group crash-landed after sustaining flak damage during a strafing of Chateaudun airdrome in France. The pilot was 1st Lt. Kenneth R. Williams. The Germans have draped the plane with netting for camouflage. (USAF)

A Flying Fortress that came down in occupied territory was partially dismantled and trucked away by the Germans. They managed to get at least one of every Eighth Air Force type for evaluation. (USAF)

A direct hit in the bomb bay over Merseburg almost destroyed this B-17G of the 92nd Bomb Group. It tore a gaping hole in the right side of the fuselage, and threw the aircraft into a wallowing dive. As pilot, Lt. Bosko struggled to regain control; a fire fed by hydraulic fluid burned at insulation, and the No. 3 engine was lost. The rest of the crew battled the fire, assisted the wounded, and worked to defuse the bomb load. They limped back to Woodbridge with two dead and several injured. (USAF)

This was an all too frequent scene on the airfields and landing grounds of England in World War II. Medics tend to a B-17 crewmember just back from a mission over enemy territory. Bombers with wounded aboard would fire a red flare and get priority in landing. (USAF)

When battle-damaged bombers had wounded aboard who could not parachute, belly landings were attempted. Crewmembers always considered a belly landing less risky than a parachute jump. This B-17G of the 525th Squadron, 379th Bomb Group makes a nice belly flop at Kimbolton, England. It was repaired and put back in service, only to be lost over Germany in September 1944. (USAF)

This B-17 of the 388th Bomb Group crashed and burned in England after delivering her crew back to base. (USAF)

A B-24 of the 392nd Bomb Group, damaged by flak, peels out of formation near Pas de Calais and heads for England. (USAF)

With the hydraulic system shot out, the crew of this 784th Squadron B-24 improvised with parachute brakes, and landed safely at the 466th Bomb Group's base, Attlebridge, England. (USAF)

The start of a mission could be as dangerous as the air over enemy territory. This scene of devastation at Podington, England, is the aftermath of a three-plane collision in early morning mist with poor visibility. The 92nd Bomb Group B-17s were loaded with bombs and gasoline. Twenty-one crewmembers were killed and several were injured. (USAF)

Fighter pilots also encountered inherent risks at takeoff. A crash in a fuel-laden P-47 killed Lt. Archie Daniels, 83rd Squadron, 78th Fighter Group. (Lambert)

Capt. Robert Stultz and his crew chief, S/Sgt. Clarence Greer, examine battle damage to the tail of a 20th Fighter Group P-38. (Bob Foose)

The canopy of Lt. Jack Martin's P-38 was holed by shrapnel dangerously close to the pilot's head. He served with the 20th Fighter Group. (Bob Foose)

"Sirocco," a B-17F, No. 42-30334, was one of the pioneers of the Eighth Air Force. She flew with the 97th Bomb Group on the earliest missions of 1942, then the group transferred to North Africa. She appears here late in the Mediterranean campaign looking worn and patched. After a major depot overhaul the Fortress was transferred back to the Eighth and the 390th Bomb Group, serving under the names "Virgin Sturgeon" and "Eight Ball." Her string ran out on 29 January 1944 over Frederichshafen, Germany, when she was shot down and crashed in Lake Constance. The entire crew became POWs. (Bill Hess)

"Delayed Action," No. 42-100117, served with the 579th Squadron, 392nd Bomb Group. It was lost on 18 March 1944. On that date other elements of the 2nd Air Division aborted or turned back for one reason or another. The 392nd soldiered on alone to the assigned target at Frederichshafen, Germany. They encountered flak, and then 60-75 single-engine German fighters attacking in line abreast. The 392nd suffered 14 B-24s lost over Europe, and one was wrecked on crash landing. Seven aircraft returned to Wendling, England, with dead and wounded aboard. (USAF)

The lettering on this veteran B-17 says, "Duffy's Tavern, J. Locher, Prop." 1st Lt. J. Locher, 527th Squadron, 379th Bomb Group poses. Note there are two bullet or flak holes visible on the Fort. Locher flew his quota of missions and survived the war, but his B-17 did not. She was lost on 29 January 1944 with another crew. (USAF)

A B-17 plunges to its death over Chateaudun, France, on 28 March 1944. A direct hit by AA fire caused the loss of this 452nd Bomb Group aircraft. When a direct hit sent a bomber spinning out of control, centrifugal force usually pinned the crew in the wreckage, preventing the opportunity to parachute. (USAF)

Belly landing a battle-damaged aircraft was common, as seen in the photos herein. However, for a smooth slide with the least amount of danger the protruding ball turret had to be retracted or jettisoned. When the turret of "Carolina Queen," 381st Bomb Group, would not retract, the crew and those at their Ridgewell base had to adapt. The B-17, piloted by 2nd Lt Leslie Bond, had its hydraulic system damaged, and the crew was unable to lower the gear. Nor could they detach the ball turret. Another B-17 took off from Ridgewell with a special tool for the job. The second B-17, piloted by Lt. Col. Conway Hall, flew just above "Carolina Queen," lowering the needed tool on a rope. Sgt. W.R. Jones, leaning into the slipstream through a window, snared it. Minus the ball turret, Bond brought her in for this landing. (USAF)

Capt. Duane Beeson, 334th Squadron, 4th Fighter Group, was a 17-victory ace. He had a narrow escape from disaster in March 1944 when German AA ventilated the tail of his Mustang. Just a few days later he ran out of luck, and flak damage forced him to crash land near Berlin. He became a POW. (USAF)

"Bottle Baby," a B-24J of the 858th Bomb Squadron, was lost during the Politz refinery mission of 20 June 1944. The crew of Lt. Goodridge was either killed or made POWs. This was one of 14 Libs from the 492nd Bomb Group that was lost on this date. The 492nd lost 55 aircraft and 520 men during 67 missions over 89 days and was withdrawn from combat. (USAF)

Lt. Furnace brought his flak damaged "Shack Rat" back to the 466th Bomb Group's base at Attlebridge, England, on two engines with no hydraulics for a crosswind landing. The B-24H was damaged beyond repair, but the crew survived. (USAF)

Crewmen of the 379th Bomb Group examine the gaping flak hole in their B-17 back at base in Kimbolton, England. (USAF)

1st Lt. Tom Murphy, 791st Squadron, 467th Bomb Group, was piloting "Stinger" on a mission to Brunswick, Germany, when enemy fighters hit the formation. His B-24 sustained major damage, but he got it back to England, only to find that the right landing gear would not extend fully. Rather than expose his crew to a difficult crash landing, he ordered them to bail out over the base at Rackheath. Then, alone, he set the Lib down for the best possible one gear crash landing. (USAF)

A German 88 mm shell tore away the nose of "Lil' Satan," a B-17 of the 379th Bomb Group. With a mortally wounded bombardier aboard, the pilot brought the aircraft home from France for an emergency landing at RAF Hunsden. (USAF)

A direct hit by German AA near Fallerslaben sent "Little Warrior" down on 29 June 1944. The aircraft commander was Lt. John Hansen of the 493rd Bomb Group. The B-24H, No. 42-94812, is seen here just seconds before its death dive. The entire crew was killed. (USAF)

Badly damaged during a raid on Munich, this B-17G of the 350th Squadron, 100th Bomb Group attempted a crash landing in Switzerland, hitting a Swiss railroad power line and causing a fire. Pilot 2nd Lt. Donald Waters and other crewmembers survived and were interned. (Bob Foose)

"Umbriago," Liberator No. 44-40068, 859th Squadron, 492nd Bomb Group, flies through flak toward a target in Saarbrucken, Germany, on 16 July 1944. She was lost on 17 February 1945 while serving with the 467th Bomb Group. (USAF)

The crew of 1st Lt. Ronald J. Nichols poses in front of "Just Plain Lonesome," No. 42-39975. They completed their missions with the 323rd Squadron, 91st Bomb Group, and returned to the States. But the B-17G was lost over Belgium on 30 May 1944 with the crew of 1st Lt. Zack Collier. (USAF)

While bombing targets in the Pas de Calais area, "Queen of Hearts" received flak damage that obliged her pilot to make a rough landing. Note that the tire on the nose wheel was torn off. The Lib had completed 25 missions and downed six German fighters according to the symbols under the pilot's window. Shrapnel holes are visible here and there. The radioman was killed, and two others were wounded. The Lib served with the 786th Squadron, 466th Bomb Group. (USAF)

The "Chow Hound," a B-17G (No. 42-31367) of the 322nd Squadron, 91st Bomb Group, plows on toward the Erkner ball bearing factory on 8 March 1944. She was lost with the entire crew of 1st Lt. Jack R. Thompson near Caen, France, in August 1944. (USAF)

This B-17G made it back to England in damaged condition, and had to crash land at Bassingbourn, England. The damage was repaired, and she went back into service with the 324th Squadron, 91st Bomb Group. However, the Fortress and crew were not as lucky twice. She was lost over the Continent on 16 August 1944. (USAF)

"Chicago Gun Moll," a P-51B of the 362nd Fighter Squadron, 357th Fighter Group is admired by its pilot, Capt. Robert D. Brown, and the ground crew. Bombs painted on the fuselage indicate missions flown, and the two swastikas represent victory claims. On 13 September 1944 Brown was a claim for some German fighter pilot. His plane was damaged, and he parachuted to land in Switzerland. (USAF)

"Texas Ranger" was a P-51B also with the357th Fighter Group. It was downed on 28 September 1944, and pilot Lt. John S. Templin became a POW. The Mustang was a C model with a British modified "Malcolm" hood over the cockpit. (Merle Olmsted)

A flak burst demolished the nose of this B-17 over Cologne, Germany, on 15 October 1944, killing both the navigator and bombardier. Despite this seemingly mortal damage the pilot, 1st Lt. Lawrence M. DeLancey, brought her home to the 398th Bomb Group's base at Nuthampstead, England. (USAF)

The 364th Fighter Group was escorting bombers over Hamburg when they got into a brawl with German fighters. Cannon hits nearly tore the tail off this Mustang, but the 385th Squadron pilot brought it home to Honington. (USAF).

On 2 November 1944 over 1,000 Eighth Air Force bombers hit targets in Germany. The 3rd Air Division concentrated on the oil refinery at Merseburg. Forty B-17s and B-24s were lost to flak and fighters. Here the B-17 of Lt. David Paris, 834th Squadron, 486th Bomb Group is seen falling, minus its nose section, with a sheet of flames trailing the wreckage. None of the crew survived. In a direct hit some crew were killed instantly, and some were blown free of the aircraft without their parachutes. Those trapped in the wreckage rarely had the opportunity to don their chutes and jump. (USAF)

A whimsical "Man O'War," No. 42-380083 poses with the crew of 1st Lt. William S. Burtt from the 322nd Squadron, 91st Bomb Group. They completed their combat tour and rotated. The B-17G was lost with another crew over Merseburg, Germany, on 2 November 1944. (USAF)

During a raid on Cologne, bombs from a high squadron fell on the nose of the B-17G "Hell's Angel." One smashed through the astrodome, and two hit the Plexiglas nose. The navigator, Lt. Leroy Drummond, was killed, but the pilot, Lt. Floyd Metts, managed to fly the damaged Fort back to the 381st Bomb Group's base at Ridgewell. (USAF)

On 26 November 1944 energetic German defenses cost the Eighth Air Force 34 bombers during a raid on Hanover. "Dorty Treek," a B-24J of the 853rd Squadron, was one of 15 Liberators lost from the 491st Bomb Group. The aircraft commander was Lt. Butler. (USAF)

German oil production was under attack again on 30 November 1944 by over 1,200 Eighth Air Force heavies. German flak and fighters took a toll of 28 B-17s, including this one from the 487th Bomb Group. She was hit in a fuel tank, and all crewmembers were believed lost. (USAF)

The 3rd Air Division wades through a sea of high-caliber shell bursts near Politz, Germany. Each harmless looking puff of smoke produced a blizzard of killing shrapnel. The nearest bursts would rock the four-engine heavies with concussion. This is the view out the waist gun window of a B-17. (USAF)

A B-17G of the 95th Bomb Group fights its way home from a mission to northern Germany on 11 April 1944. Note the damage to the wing from Luftwaffe attackers. The tail gunner is still fending off enemy fighters. "Thomper" flew many more missions, but was lost in November over Merseburg with five crew killed and four POWs. (USAF)

After the Augsburg raid of 13 April 1944, this B-17G of the 339th Squadron, 96th Bomb Group was forced to land in Dubendorf, Switzerland, because of battle damage. The pilot was 2nd Lt. William C. Potter. The Swiss Air Force repaired the Fort, and used it for interception exercises with Swiss fighters. (Bob Foose)

The neutral Swiss also acquired a few P-51 Mustangs that were unable to return to Allied territory because of battle damage. (USAF)

Over 1,000 Eighth Air Force bombers and over 600 fighters were above Germany on 29 January 1945. This B-17 from the 379th Bomb Group was hit by flak and its No. 3 engine caught fire. Pilot 2nd Lt. Newton Kerr sent the plane into a dive that put out the fire, which burned both wing and tail control surfaces. He landed at an Allied base on the Continent. (USAF)

"Lady Be Good" was attacked by Me. 262 jets over Berlin on 3 February 1945 and sustained major damage. The pilot, 1st Lt. Craig P. Greason, managed to set the 457th Bomb Group B-17G down in liberated Belgium. (USAF)

The crew of this 92nd Bomb Group B-17 is amazed at its good fortune, as they view battle damage that nearly took off the left half of the tail. They had just returned safely from a 9 February 1945 mission bombing the synthetic oil refinery at Lutzkendorff, Germany. (USAF)

On 18 March 1945 over 1,100 bombers attacked Berlin. The Germans mounted a spirited defense, although the end of the war was less than two months away. Thirteen bombers were lost over the target area, and 15 others sustained major damage. Over 700 received minor damage, and six escorting fighters were lost. This 401st Bomb Group Fortress made it back to England despite a gaping flak wound in the left wing tip. A few feet further to the right and the shell would have hit a fuel tank. The pilot was 2nd Lt. Cameron. (USAF)

Just a month from the end of the war German defenses could still dish out punishment. The B-17 "Wee Willie" of the 91st Bomb Group is torn apart by a direct hit over Berlin. Some of the crew of 1st Lt. Robert Fuller managed to escape the twisting wreck to become POWs. (USAF)

During a raid on Kiel, Germany, the 34th Bomb Group encountered stiff resistance. Of the 35 attackers, three were lost and 15 suffered major battle damage, and nearly every B-24 was hit. They brought home five wounded. One of those Liberators that did not return was "The Near Sighted Robin," No. 41-28851. With its #4 engine feathered, the pilot sought sanctuary in Sweden. (Ed Kueppers)

Me. 262s attacked the 2nd Air Division on 4 April 1945 and downed this 448th Bomb Group Liberator in northwest Germany. On this day the Eighth Air Force put nearly 1,000 bombers and over 800 fighters over Germany. (USAF)

On 17 April 1945 Lt. Col. Elwyn Righetti, Commanding Officer of the 55th Fighter Group, was shot down by German light AA guns while strafing an airdrome near Dresden. Post war investigations led to the belief that German civilians killed him after he crash-landed. (John Gray)

A large caliber AA shell burst beneath this 91st Bomb Group B-17, almost severing the fuselage. Shrapnel caused several casualties. (Bob Foose)

6

The Results

Military historians still argue as to whether or not air power was decisive in the defeat of Germany. It took ground forces on two fronts to finally penetrate the Reich and conclusively defeat the German army. However, the strategic bombing campaign by the Allies over some three years finally had the cumulative effect of wrecking much of German industry. Fighting the combined bomber offensive was a war of attrition that the Luftwaffe ultimately lost. By 1945 the Allies had wrested control of the air from the Germans, and its heavy bomber fleets were destroying both industrial and urban centers almost at will.

Just a month before the German surrender of 8 May 1945, when it was apparent that the end was near, the chiefs of the combined bomber offensive became concerned that continued destruction of German cities would hamper occupation forces. The RAF ceased its area bombing campaign, and the Eighth Air Force all but terminated strategic air strikes, concentrating largely on airdromes and tactical support of ground forces.

The scenes in this chapter are only representative of the massive destruction wrought by the bombers. Since the Fifteenth Air Force and the RAF often visited some of the same targets, the damages, in some cases, may be the result of combined and repeated attacks.

Actual strike photos were taken at high altitude during missions. Some photos that do not show fires or smoke may be reconnaissance photos taken for evaluation before and after missions. Those pictures taken at much lower altitudes, and the few from ground level, were made after the end of hostilities.

A low altitude photo of the Merseburg Luena synthetic oil refinery, just two weeks after the German surrender, shows its almost complete destruction from repeated air raids. (USAF)

After the fires have died, ground level photos of Merseburg (above and below) provide more detail on the effect of bombing. (USAF)

The Buer-Schloven refinery at Gelsenkirchen is devastated by repeated bombings. It was one of the main sources for aviation fuel. (USAF)

This bizarre concrete dome that stood in the midst of the destruction at Gelsenkirchen was an air raid shelter for the refinery's skilled technicians. (USAF)

Before and after photos of a synthetic oil plant at Misburg, near Hanover. (Above) The vast complex as it appeared to air reconnaissance in mid-1944. (Below) The plant had been largely flattened in September 1944 by repeated bombing strikes. Note the array of round bomb craters in the area surrounding the plant proper. (both USAF)

The city of Cologne, Germany, is silent at the end of the war. Its great cathedral was spared, but the railway station, right of the church, was hit, and both rail and highway bridge spans over the Rhine were destroyed. (Sam Sox)

An electric generating plant at Knappsack, Germany, was bombed out of business. (Sam Sox)

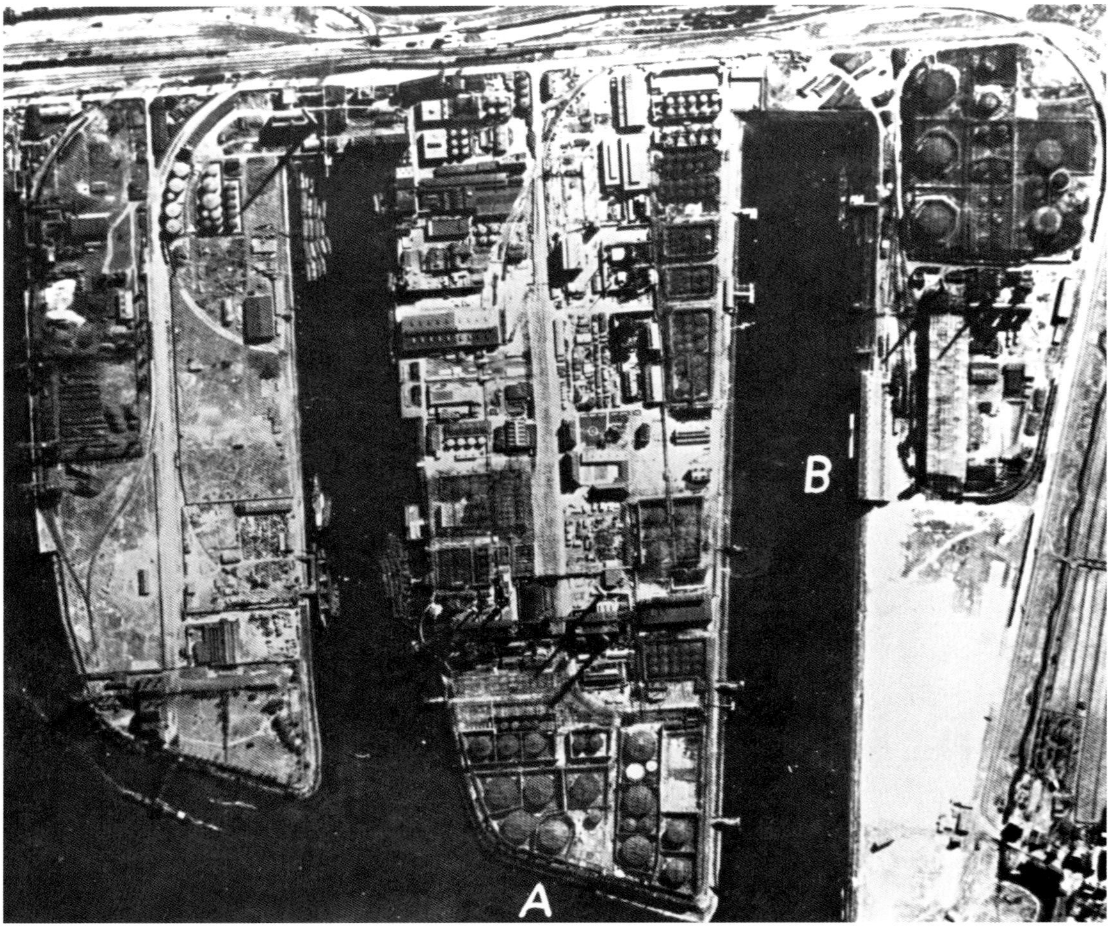

Harburg was a bustling seaport and industrial complex on the Elbe estuary, across the river from Hamburg. (USAF)

This photo, taken after VE-Day, focuses on the peninsula of land corresponding to "A" in the photo above. It is a scene of utter destruction created by Eighth Air Force bombing. (USAF)

In a pockmarked landscape, craters and gutted tanks are all that remain of a vast petro-chemical complex at Ruhland, Germany. (USAF)

It wasn't exactly the "bomb in the pickle barrel" that Air Force bomber adherents had predicted. However, this bombing of the Europaische Tankerlager crude oil refinery at Hamburg in June 1944 laid the bulk of its ordnance on the target without touching the residential area to the right. Portions of the refinery at the top are burning furiously, while bombs from a new wave of attackers can be seen striking below. (USAF)

German movement of men, materiel, and supplies by rail was hampered, and then almost totally halted by continuous attacks on major transportation arteries. This is a marshalling yard at Frieberg, Germany, near the close of the war. The destruction of railways and highway bridges ultimately paralyzed the German Army. (USAF)

The immense I.G. Farben chemical plant at Ludwigshafen is silent by May 1945. (USAF)

The Luftwaffe was pursued relentlessly in the air and on the ground. A Focke-Wulf 190, carrying a drop tank, is lit up by the gunfire of 2nd Lt. Edison Stiff, a P-47 pilot of the 352nd Squadron, 353rd Fighter Group. It was scored as probably destroyed. (USAF)

Capt. James Dalglish of the 354th Fighter Group hits a FW 190, and catches a view of the pilot as he parachutes. (USAF)

A P-47 pilot of the 56th Fighter Group brazenly duels a flak tower in occupied France. (USAF)

Lt. Ernest Lang, 84th Squadron, 78th Fighter Group peppers a twin-engine Potez 63 at a German airdrome in France as another P-47 strafer is caught in the gun camera lens. (USAF)

After escorting 1st Air Division B-17s to Lutzkendorff, Mustangs of the 20th Fighter Group swept down line abreast to strafe Esperstedt Airdrome on 9 February 1945. They left 34 enemy aircraft burning, and the scene was recorded in this remarkable view. No P-51s were lost. (USAF)

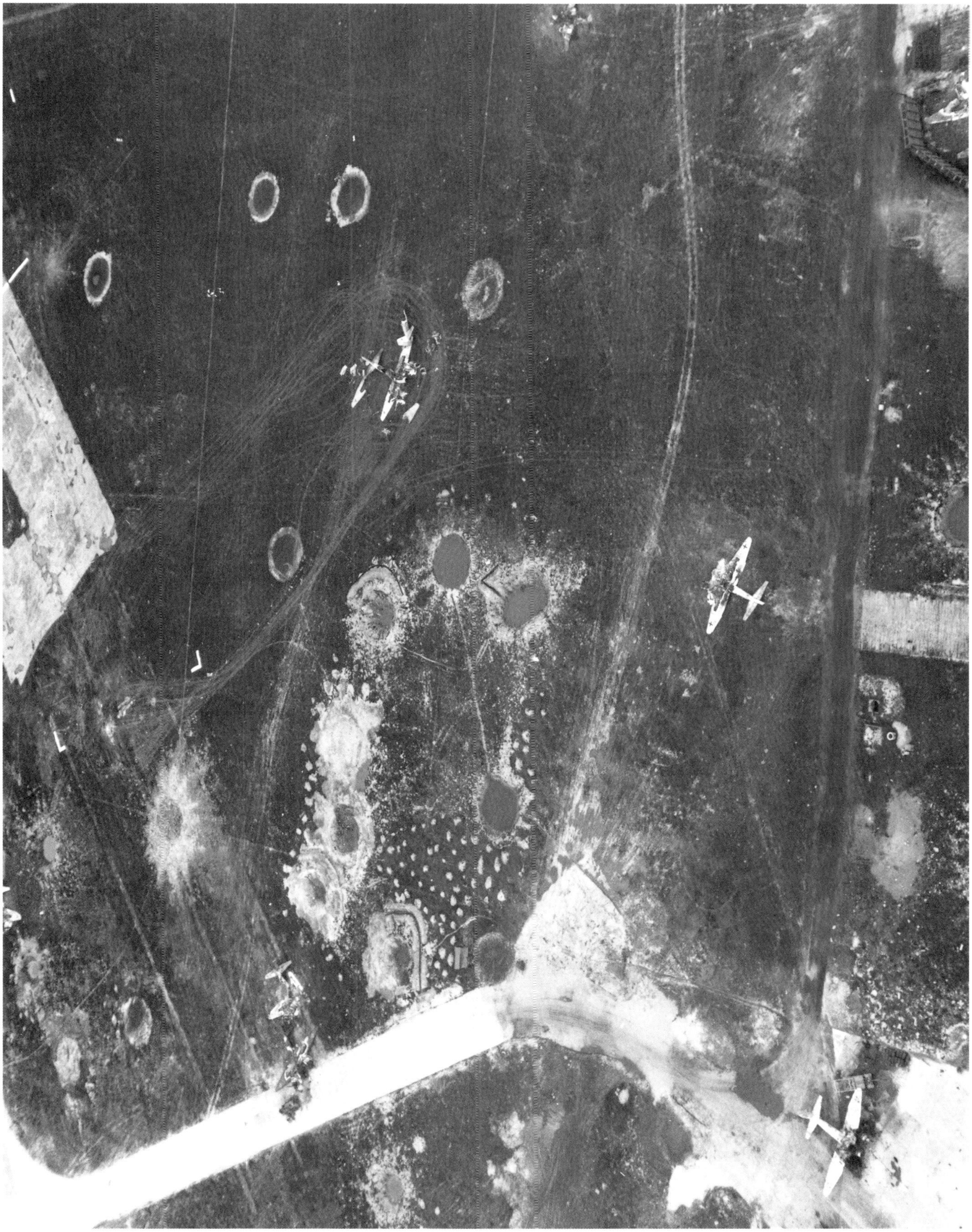

By 10 April 1945, less than a month before the German surrender, there was hardly anything worth strafing as the 55th Fighter Group visited this cratered airdrome near Nauhoff. Every enemy plane in view had previously been burned. (USAF)

Unfortunate timing: a Junkers 52 transport lands at a German airfield that has come under strafing attack by 8th Fighter Command. It crashed and burned seconds later. (USAF)

This is the view from the gun camera of Maj. George E. Preddy, Jr., a P-51 ace from the 352nd Fighter Group, as he sweeps at treetop level over a German airfield. The twin-engine bomber that is absorbing his .50 caliber fire is a Heinkel 177. Preddy was later killed in action. (USAF)

Below: The architect of Eighth Air Force strategy from January 1944 to VE-Day, 8 May 1945, was Lt. Gen. Jimmy Doolittle (left), one of America's most distinguished aviators. He had led the Tokyo raid in 1942. After the German surrender he set off for Okinawa to command units of the Eighth Air Force that would form there to pursue the war with Japan. (USAF)

7

Warbird Profiles

It is said that decorating military equipment and machines goes back to antiquity. Certainly the practice with aircraft began in the first air war, World War I. The Germans and the RAF also painted names and symbols on their aircraft, but the Americans in every theatre of war elevated it to an art form during the '40s.

The names that American airmen applied to their machines were frequently wives, girl friends, song titles, and comic strip characters. But there were a variety of whimsical names, a lot of black humor, and poetic names for imaginary sexy ladies. In most cases U.S. Army Air Force crews went beyond simply naming a bomber. Artwork that expanded on the name or theme was common, and as time went on some efforts produced massive murals. Fighters were also named, but their smaller frames did not present the broad expanse that lured the G.I. artists.

The names or themes and the accompanying artwork were the product of individual pilots or crew inspiration. Army officialdom did not sanction, but rather tolerated aircraft art, recognizing it as a morale booster.

"Nose art," as it became commonly known, was created largely by ground crew members who were commercial artists or frustrated painters. Many of the ladies portrayed on bombers were copied from Esquire magazine, the work of professional artists like Alberto Vargas, George Petty, and others. It was their contribution to the war effort.

The motivation to name an 18-ton aircraft and fashion a piece of artwork was largely a matter of pride in one's effort or military profession—*esprit de corps*. Your aircraft became an entity, like a ship. Just as no cavalryman would ride into battle on a mount called "horse," it didn't do much for morale to call your airplane No. 793. A name and appropriate picture established a closer association to the crew.

On these pages we present a collection of bomber nose art in both color and black and white. We wish that more color had survived, but it seems that WWII was largely a black and white war. Where available, we include aircraft serial numbers for the avid history buff or veterans' families. The individual serial number can be useful in tracking "Missing Air Crew Reports" through U.S. Air Force historical archives.

"Old 66" was a B-17F veteran of the 561st Squadron, 388th Bomb Group. It survived over 60 missions, and was retired at Knettishall, England, to be cannibalized. (USAF)

"Sweetheart," No. 42-3262, was a B-17F that flew a lot of missions with the 561st Squadron, 388th Bomb Group, and always returned. (USAF)

"Ol' Man Tucker" was a B-17G (No. 42-38004) with the 534th Squadron, 381st Bomb Group. It was lost during a raid on Eschwege, Germany, in April 1944. (USAF)

During the Bremen mission of 26 November 1943 "Tiger Girl," B-17G No. 42-3555, collided with another B-17, and the crew perished. It served with the 560th Squadron, 388th Bomb Group. (USAF)

"Stage Door Canteen," a B-17G (No. 42-31990), survived the war after many missions with the 535th Squadron, 381st Bomb Group. Visiting celebrities in England were often photographed with the Fort. (USAF)

The B-17G "Shark Tooth," appears to have a bone in its teeth as it gnaws on the chin turret. No. 42-32012 served with the 614th Squadron, 401st Bomb Group (USAF)

"E-rat-icator," a B-17G (No. 42-39970), survived over 100 missions with the 730th Squadron, 452nd Bomb Group. (USAF)

"Thunder Bird," shown here with its proud ground crew, was retired after 100 successful missions with the 359th Squadron, 303rd Bomb Group. A B-17G (No. 42-38050), it was the first in the outfit to arrive in NMF. The aircrew thought that it stood out from the other olive drab Forts and might attract German fighters, so they had her painted. (USAF)

"Bonnie" flew with the 784th Squadron, 466th Bomb Group. She was a B-24H, No. 41-29459. (USAF)

"Joanne" was a B-17G (No. 42-97174) with the 534th Squadron, 381st Bomb Group. She was lost on the Berlin mission of 21 June 1944. The entire crew of Lt. Roger Dussault became POWs. (USAF)

Lt. Bill von Platten crash-landed his B-17G, No. 43-37899, at Sudberry, England, in bad weather. "Rack and Ruin" was repaired and flew again. (USAF)

"Phyllis," a B-17G (No. 42-31067), completed many missions for the 535th Squadron, 381st Bomb Group, bringing all her crews back to England. She was retired, and returned to the States in late 1944. (USAF)

(Above) Even the tails of some B-17s got the shark-nosed paint job usually reserved for the nose, as seen here at the aft end of a 306th Bomb Group B-17 and its twin.50-caliber stinger. (Below) The crew of "Princess Pat," 358th Squadron, 303rd Bomb Group, musters for a photo near the tail turret of their Fortress. (USAF)

This B-24H was with the 329th Squadron, 93rdBomb Group. t had no name but the full lion's head paint job. (USAF)

"Rose of Juarez," (foreground) a B-24H, No. 42-7469, of the 579th Squadron, 392nd Bomb Group, is a relatively late model with the darker OD paint job. The sister Liberator is an obvious veteran with its faded olive drab. They are over the coast of Kent. (USAF)

On 20 February 1944 the B-17G "Lackin' Shackin'" heads toward Leipzig, Germany. FW 190s shot her down on 11 April 1944 near Stettin, Germany, with the crew of Lt. F.C. Amman. (USAF)

"Elflako" of the 735th Squadron, 453rd Bomb Group, was a B-24H. Damaged over enemy territory, its crew was obliged to ditch in the North Sea in May 1944. RAF crash boats rescued them. (USAF)

"Duration Plus" was a B-17G (No. 42-31726) of the 367th Squadron, 306th Bomb Group. It was lost over Germany on 13 September 1944. (USAF)

"Irish Lassie," a B-17G (No. 44-8475), was with the 322nd Squadron, 91st Bomb Group. (USAF)

"Unavailable Mable" was nose art in stark contrast with the other chicks of the Eighth Bomber Command. A B-17G (No. 42-97397), Mable flew with the 423rd Squadron, 306th Bomb Group. (USAF)

"Paper Doll" was a popular tune of the '40s. The B-17G was with the 423rd Squadron, 306th Bomb Group. (USAF)

"Corky," a B-24H (No. 42-52234), served with two units, the 446th and the 453rd Bomb Groups. (Bob Foose)

"Mist'er Choice" was a B-24H (No. 41-28691) with the 785th Squadron, 466th Bomb Group. (Bob Foose)

"Herk's Jerks," B-24J No. 44-40125, was with the 858th Squadron, 492nd Bomb Group. (USAF)

"Tarfu II," (No. 42-106425) a B-24J, served in the 448th Bomb Group. Note how some crewmen have named their respective spaces. Jim Daugherty was the pilot. (Ed Kueppers)

During a deep penetration mission to Brux, Czechoslovakia, in September 1944, the 306th Bomb Group lost eight B-17Gs, three shown here: "Belle of the Blue," No. 42-102503; "Tailwind," No. 42-97368; and "Methuselah," No. 42-102969. (Bob Foose)

"Bomber Dear," a B-17G (No. 42-97234) of the 322nd Squadron, 91st Bomb Group, was lost retiring from Merseburg on 2 November 1944. She lagged behind the squadron and was set upon by fighters. The pilot was Lt. Sparkman. The artist for this and other 322nd Forts was Cpl. Tony Starcer. (USAF)

"She Devil" was a B-24J, No. 44-40123, with the 852nd Squadron, 491st Bomb Group. (USAF)

In November 1944 "Lady Jane" was forced down in Holland because of flak damage, and the crew was captured. A B-17G, No. 42-107009, she flew with the 613th Squadron, 401st Bomb Group. (USAF)

"Ikky Poo" was a B-17G (No. 42-31760) with the 334th Squadron, 95th bomb Group. With Lt. McVay as aircraft commander, it was lost over the Continent on 6 November 1944. Some of the crew was captured, but others evaded. (USAF)

On 10 November 1944 "Red Ass" is seen en route to Hanau, Germany. A B-24H (No. 42-95203), she belonged to the 706th Squadron, 446th Bomb Group. (USAF)

Ready for a mission, the crew of B-17G No. 43-37704 "Button Nose" gathers to check the mission map at Ridgewell. They were members of the 535th Squadron, 381st Bomb Group. Both aircraft and crew survived the war. (USAF)

"Sweet Moonbeam McSwine," No. 42-95710, was a character from Al Capp's Dogpatch cartoons. She graced the side of this B-24H of the 704th Squadron, 446th Bomb Group. (Ed Kueppers)

"Hell and Back," a B-24H (No. 42-95170), served with the 493rd Bomb Group. (Ed Kueppers)

"Johnny Come Lately" salvoes a load of bombs over a German target. A B-24J (No. 42-110154), she flew with the 855th Squadron, 491st Bomb Group. (USAF)

A B-17G, No. 44-6104 "Homing Pigeon," served with the 613th Squadron, 401st Bomb Group. She was one of 25 bombers lost in attacks on Germany on 21 November 1944. (USAF)

The B-24J (No. 44-40475) named "Jolly Roger" served with the 752nd Squadron, 458th Bomb Group. (USAF)

"Dolly's Sister" was damaged during a 21 November 1944 raid on Hamburg. The pilot of the B-24H, 734th Squadron, 453rd Bomb Group judged that he could not return to England, and aborted to Sweden. (Bob Foose)

This B-17G, No. 42-31515, crash landed in England as a result of battle damage. "The Wild Hare" was destroyed, but had brought its crew home safely. Pilot was Lt. B.V. Parsons. (USAF)

"Little Guy" was downed over Germany on 26 November 1944, and the crew of 1st Lt. Kyle Smith became POWs. She served with the 532nd Squadron, 381st Bomb Group. (USAF)

B-17G No. 42-97313 of the 535th Squadron, 381st Bomb Group was damaged over Germany on 14 January 1945, and pilot 2nd Lt. Roebuck ordered the crew to parachute. "The Columbus Miss." was over the front lines when the crew jumped. Some fell on the German side and were captured, one was killed by German ground fire as he descended, and others were rescued by Allied ground forces. (USAF)

"Fearless Fosdick" was a comic strip character. His namesake, a B-24H (No 41-29604) of the 702nd Squadron, 445th Bomb Group, appears to have slid into home. (Ed Kueppers)

The namesake of this B-24H of the 392nd bomb Group was a Red Cross worker. They met the returning crews with coffee and doughnuts at some bases. The Liberator, No. 42-50387, was lost on a Magdeburg raid early in 1945. (USAF)

"The Gremlins Roost," 579th Squadron, 392nd bomb Group, carried a lot of advertising into battle. She was a late model B-24L. (USAF)

"Little Jo," 392nd Bomb Group, ran off the runway and buried its landing gear in England's spring mud. (Bob Foose)

"Tubaro's" shark's mouth had a tongue. It was a B-24J (No. 44-40101), and served with the 854th Squadron, 491st Bomb Group. (USAF)

"Mr. Lucky" did not live up to its name. A B-17G, she served with the 550th Squadron, 385th Bomb Group. Piloted by 1st Lt. Charles Armbruster, it was involved in a collision with another Fortress over Belgium. The tail of "Mr. Lucky" was severed, and the tail gunner, Sgt. Joe F. Jones, was trapped inside the twisting descending hulk. Somehow the tail section fluttered rather than crashed to earth, and Belgian citizens extricated Sgt. Jones, who survived his 13,000-foot descent. (USAF)

"Solid Comfort," a B-24J (No. 42-50501), belonged to the 330th Squadron, 93rd Bomb Group. (USAF)

This B-24J of the 753rd Squadron, 458th Bomb Group had no visible name, but bore a lion's head design, a variation on the oft-used shark-nosed figure. (USAF)

A late model B-24M No. 44-50532, named "Greaser" (name not visible), of the 853rd Squadron, 491st Bomb Group, participates in one of the last missions of the war. The Alps are in the background. (Bob Foose)

EIGHTH AIR FORCE

BOMBARDMENT GROUPS

1st Bombardment Division				2nd Bombardment Division				3rd Bombardment Division			
1st Wing	40th Wing	41st Wing	94th Wing	2nd Wing	14th Wing	20th Wing	96th Wing	4th Wing	13th Wing	45th Wing	93rd Wing
91st BG	92nd BG	303rd BG	351st BG	389th BG	44th BG	93rd BG	458th BG	94th BG	95th BG	96th BG	34th BG
381st BG	305th BG	379th BG	401st BG	445th BG	392nd BG	446th BG	466th BG	447th BG	100th BG	388th BG	385th BG
398th BG	306th BG	384th BG	457th BG	453rd BG	491st BG	448th BG	467th BG	486th BG	390th BG	452nd BG	490th BG
Assoc. Units:		801st BG	482nd BG		492nd BG	489th BG		487th BG			493rd BG

FIGHTER GROUPS

1st Bombardment Division	2nd Bombardment Division	3rd Bombardment Division
67th Fighter Wing	65th Fighter Wing	66th Fighter Wing
20th FG	4th FG	55th FG
352nd FG	56th FG	78th FG
356th FG	355th FG	339th FG
359th FG	361st FG	353rd FG
364th FG	479th FG	357th FG

"V-mail," a B-17F (No. 42-30451), flew with the 423rd Squadron, 306th Bomb Group. (Bob Foose)

B-17G No. 42-31767, "Our gal Sal," was with the 351st Squadron, 100th Bomb Group. (Bob Foose)

"Mason and Dixon" was a B-17G of the 351st Squadron, 100th Bomb Group. (Bob Foose)

"Cock O' the Sky" flew 110 missions without an abort. She was a B-17G (No. 42-102668) with the 710th Squadron, 447th Bomb Group. (Bob Foose)

"Rum Runner," a B-24H (No. 42-52496), flew with the 34th and later the 493rd Bomb Group. (Bob Foose)

"Flying Jenny" was a B-17G (No. 42-37722) with the 350th Squadron, 100th Bomb Group. (Bob Foose)

B-17F No. 42-31066 flew with the 351st Squadron, 100th Bomb Group. She was lost near Hamburg on 31 December 1944. Six killed and three POWs. (Bob Foose)

"Naughty Nancy" was a B-17G (No. 43-39116) with the 423rd Squadron, 306th Bomb Group. (Bob Foose)

A B-24J (No. 44-40298) was adorned with a beauty later covered over by the field installation of armor plate just below the pilot's window. She first flew with the 458th Bomb Group, and then the 487th. (Bob Foose)

"Lay or Bust" was a B-17G (No. 42-97230) with the 418th Squadron, 100th Bomb Group. (Bob Foose)

"Body Sox," a B-17G (No. 44-8158), served with the 94th and 490th Bomb Group. (Bob Foose)

B-17G No. 43-38138, "Ole' Timer," was with the 4th Squadron, 34th Bomb Group. (Bob Foose)

The B-17G "Boss Lady," No. 42-102611, was lost in weather over the North Sea on 27 June 1944, taking with it the entire crew from the 350th Squadron, 100th Bomb Group. (Bob Foose)

"Blonde Bomber II," a B-17G (No. 43-38524), served with the 710th Squadron, 447th Bomb Group. (Bob Foose)

"Cancer" was adorned on B-24H No. 42-52650. (Bob Foose)

Philip S. Brinkman, a commercial artist in the 834th Squadron, 486th Bomb Group, performed the nose art on this and the facing page Liberators of the 834th. "Leo II" is B-24H No. 42-52768. (Bob Foose)

"Aries," B-24H No. 42-52765, with artist Brinkman at work. (Bob Foose)

"Virgo," B-24H No. 42-52532. All of these bombers, named for Zodiac characters, survived the war. (Bob Foose)

B-24J No. 44-40440, named "Lil Hoot," served with the 493rd Bomb Group. (Bob Foose)

"Queenie," a B-17G (No. 43-38332), served with the 34th Bomb Group, and had completed over 75 missions at the time of this photo. (Bob Foose)

The B-17G No. 44-8271, "Butch," flew with the 39 st Squadron, 34th Bomb Group. (Bob Foose)

"D-Day Doll," a B-17G (No. 43-37544), flew many missions with the 710th Squadron, 447th Bomb Group. (Bob Foose)

B-24H No. 42-94789, named "Merchant," was lost in a mid-air collision over Normandy on D-Day, 6 June 1944. She was assigned to the 862nd Squadron, 493rd Bomb Group. (Bob Foose)

B-24H No. 42-52759, "Big Dealer," 862nd Squadron, 493rd Bomb Group, was lost over France on 22 June 1944. (Bob Foose)

"Knockout Dropper" (No. 44-8731), a B-17G with the 4th Squadron, 34th Bomb Group. (Bob Foose)

B-17G No. 42-97280, "Haybag Annie," was with the 550th Squadron. 385th Bomb Group. (Bob Foose)

"Katrinka" was with the 863rd Squadron, 493rd Bomb Group. She was a B-24H, No. 42-51197. (Bob Foose)

"Shady Lady" was lost on 31 March 1945 over Brunswick, Germany, while serving with the 566th Squadron, 389th Bomb Group. It was a B-24J, No. 44-40439. (Bob Foose)

B-24H No. 42-94828, "You're Safe at Home," was with the 490th Bomb Group. (Bob Foose)

"Rugged But Right," a B-24H (No. 42-94953) of the 715th Squadron, 448th Bomb Group, looked like it had been through a war. (Bob Foose)

Bibliography

Bekker, Cajus, *The Luftwaffe War Diaries*, London, England, Macdonald & Co., 1966.

Craven, Wesley F., and James L. Cate, *The Army Air forces in World War II, Volume II, Europe: Torch to Point Blank*, Chicago, Illinois, The University of Chicago Press, 1958.

Craven, Wesley F., and James L. Cate, *The Army Air Forces in World War II, Volume III, Europe: Argument to VE-Day*, Chicago, Illinois, The University of Chicago Press, 1958.

Forman, Wallace R., *B-17 Nose Art Name Directory*, North Branch, Minnesota, Specialty Press, 1996.

Forman, Wallace R., *B-24 Nose Art Name Directory*, North Branch, Minnesota, Specialty Press, 1996.

Freeman, Roger A., *The Mighty Eighth (A History of the Units, Men and Machines of the US 8th Air Force)*, Osceola, Wisconsin, Motorbooks, International, 1972.

Freeman, Roger A., with Alan Crouchman and Vic Maslen, *The Mighty Eighth War Diary*, London, England, Arms and Armour, 1990.

Kaplan, Philip, and Rex Alan Smith, *One Last Look: A Sentimental Journey to the Eighth Air Force Heavy Bomber Bases of World War II in England*, New York, New York, Abbeville Press, 1983.

Rust, Kenn C., *Eighth Air Force Story, Historical Aviation album*, Temple City, California, 1977.

Toliver, Raymond F. and Trevor J. Constable, *Fighter Aces of the Luftwaffe*, Fallbrook, California, Aero Publishers, Inc., 1977.

Vast quantities of historic data, war stories, and photos also exist for the various Eighth Air Force combat groups on their web sites, and on the site of the Mighty 8th Air Force. For those interested in researching the fate of individual personnel, the prime Internet locations are: Army Air Forces in World War II and American Battle Monuments Commission. Most but not all combat units produced unit histories. Some are currently available, but many are out of print. There is also an Eighth Air Force Historical Museum at Savannah, GA, dedicated to the preservation of World War II history.